Waking the Sleeping Church

Dr. Ralph D. Curtin

WAKING THE SLEEPING CHURCH

Endorsement

Dr. Ralph Curtin's new book, *Waking the Sleeping Church*, should be read by every pastor and church leader in America! It may be compared to the warning horn that a pilot hears when the plane is descended dangerously too low. This book alerts Christians to awaken to what they know they are witnessing today, a general malaise throughout the land—typified by what we have seen so recently; top company executives taking care of themselves instead of their employees or customers! Curtin's book strengthens our Christian prophets to summon godly courage to speak up while there is still time against the moral decay that the world is attempting to push upon the church as normal and OK.

Dr. Curtin identifies topics which people need to hear. His words are sober, yet sane, and like the letters from Christ in Revelation chapters two and three, they come with a remedy and hope. I recommend its reading, and that it be passed on to Christian leaders everywhere; not to rebuke them, but to strengthen their hands. It is a book to help American churches regain their Acts 20:20 vision: "I kept back nothing that was profitable unto you," (Paul to the Ephesian elders). –Dr. Gary G. Cohen

Dr. Gary G. Cohen is in his twenty-eighth year as professor of Biblical Studies at Trinity International University-South Florida Campus, where he now teaches in the evenings in the Excel and M.A.R. programs. He is President Emeritus of Cohen Theological Seminary, Torrance, California and Seoul, Korea. Dr. Cohen has published works of Bible commentaries and both fiction and non-fiction works.

Dr. Cohen is retired Army Reserve Chaplain (COL), and a graduate of the USAF Air War College. He has served as president of Graham Bible College and Clearwater Christian College.

Preface

Many books have been published since 9/11/01 regarding the remaking and changing of America. This publication is dedicated to the remaking and changing of the *Church* in America. When the *Church* changes, so, too, will America. Not before.

CHAPTER 1
Awakened America

Look around you and see if you can find another nation anywhere that has traded in its old gods for new ones-even though their gods are nothing . . . And yet my people have given up their glorious God for silly idols! The heavens are shocked at such a thing and shrink back in horror and dismay. For my people have done two evil things: They have forsaken me, the Fountain of Life-giving Water; and they have built for themselves broken cisterns that can't hold water!

The Prophet Jeremiah, 2:10-13 (TLB)

Imagine, if you will, that you are a Native American Mohawk Indian of yesteryear paddling your canoe down the Hudson River in modern times. Glancing around, you see oil puddles floating on the river's surface with discarded plastic soda bottles and used Pampers bobbing up and down. You look carefully along the shoreline for signs of unspoiled habitation where the eagle and the osprey use to hunt their prey, but find only abandoned automobiles and industrial

1

waste polluting the landscape. You maneuver your canoe to a small beach where you hope to find a vestige of the once-pristine land and waterways you formerly traversed, only to discover the bathers and picnickers—the generation of humankind who inherited this land from you—to be the unconcerned violators.

Tears of heartbreak would stream down your face. You would cry out, "Why have you profaned our land? How dare you abuse the natural resources we tried so hard to preserve! Is this the way you honor your god by transgressing against both divine and natural law? If this is true, then you do not deserve to live on this land."

In 629 B. C., Jeremiah brought an oracle from God to Judah in the Southern Kingdom reminding them of God's promise of protection if they obeyed His commands and observed His laws. He further reminded them that He would continue His benevolence toward them if they were compliant and sought to live as a holy nation. But Israel had forsaken the God who blessed them in favor of the pagan gods surrounding them and flagrantly flouted their sins in His face. They were not interested in turning back to the One who separated them unto Himself. Their interest was centered in the enterprise of building their nation and personal fulfillment. They were an awakened nation—awakened to the world around them with its exploration into the sciences and new-found methods for pleasure. So he sent a prophet with an endearing admonition directed at His people. His sole purpose was to turn them back to Himself once again:

Hear the word of the LORD, O house of Jacob, all you clans of the house of Israel. This is what the LORD says: What fault did your fathers find in me, that they strayed so far from me?
They followed worthless idols and became worthless themselves. I brought you into a fertile land to eat its fruit and rich produce. But you came and defiled my land and made my inheritance detestable (Jeremiah 2:4-5, 7).

How did they defile the land and become detestable in God's sight? Here are some of the charges God recited in today's vernacular language:

- Your religious leaders are not seeking after My Word or direction, but have sought their own methods of salvation and worship. They falsely promote a message of prosperity and peace when judgment is due them, 2:8.
- My people have exchanged the glory of their Hebrew heritage and followed after worthless idols of self-importance, self-aggrandizement, autonomy, materialism, hedonism, and narcissism, 2:11.
- My Name has become a byword—abused and ridiculed—being relegated to an irrelevant god, 2:19.
- You have chased after gods of wood and stone (the natural gods of this world: humanism, relativism, philosophical pluralism, existentialism), so let them save you when you are in trouble, 2:27.
- You claim that you are a religious nation, be-

ing innocent of any sin and therefore inviolable, but I will pass judgment on you for I have rejected those you trust, 2:35, 37; Lamentations 4:12.

God sent Jeremiah to give warning to Israel, but they would not hear it, being smug in their self-appointed securities. They trusted in their religious institution, their own interpretation of the Torah, and their well-constructed imposing edifices—relying on the faith of the patriarchs—not their own. But God demanded that His people put their trust in only Him, not in their organized religion. Not the wisdom of the elders, only Him. Therefore He decreed, "Your own conduct and actions have brought this upon you. This is your punishment. How bitter it is! How it pierces to the heart!" (Jeremiah 4:18). Despite Jeremiah's pleading with his people to repent and turn back to God, they would not. So God brought judgment on them by sending Arab conquerors, the ruthless and vicious Babylonian king Nebuchadnezzar with his mighty army, to destroy their strongholds and take them captive.

God's methods have not changed. He is a gracious and loving God who takes no pleasure in the destruction of earthly cities or the death of the wicked. But He is a righteous and holy God who warns His people to turn back to Him before He decrees punishment. With this measurement of historical precedence, that of God's treatment of Israel through the Babylonians, we view America's condition.

God Getting Our Attention

While it can be shown that God was dropping hints and sending signals over the past two decades displaying His grief over the way America has treated Him, on September 11, 2001, He used a "bombsight" directed at our haughty hearts and at our resolute will to get our attention. Yes, it's true that America stands as the vanguard of military supremacy, but God allowed Islamic terrorists to penetrate our defenses and crash airliners into U. S. monuments to teach us an object lesson. These monuments represent our political, economic, and military prowess. To the Bible-believing church, it was apparent that God was making a statement: You cannot put your trust in the military to protect your nation. Your trust must be in the sovereign God who superintends man's survival.

The debacle surrounding the collapse of Enron and Worldcom shortly thereafter made another deafening statement: You cannot put your trust in financial institutions. God asserted loudly and clearly that our financial and material resources come at His hand and that He can remove them very quickly; therefore, our trust must be in Him. J. Campbell White stated, "Our material resources are so stupendous that we are in danger of coming to trust in riches rather than in God."

Organized religion came next on God's list of targets. In addition to the Catholic Church scandal involving clergy abuse, Catholic Church clergy were accused of stealing millions of dollars in offerings and gifts made to their parish. In Protestant denominations, fighting emerged over homosexual ministers remaining in the church.[1]

Unfortunately, these attacks on America's fortresses have done nothing to awaken America to the real cause of our problems. As Lee Penn wrote, "If the horrors of 9/11 failed to awaken the American people to a lasting change of heart, how much *more severe* will be the events that God will allow in the future, as a final means of evoking repentance from those who are capable of it?"[2]

America has awakened in many ways, coming to the forefront of every theater of operation. We are politically, materially, financially, scientifically, sexually, emotionally awakened—even superior in many aspects—but we are *spiritually* asleep.

Relentless Eroding Of Spiritual Values

A cartoon in a recent popular magazine characterized only a fraction of America's diminishing spiritual value system. One frame of the cartoon illustrated a man raising his hand to the heavens and asking the question: "Where are all the doctors and scientists that are needed to find cures to all the diseases plaguing us?" In the next frame a voice from heaven says, "I sent them to you, but you aborted them!" Undoubtedly God is able and willing to help His creation overcome many of their medical, social, economical and political problems that assail them, but why should He? In reality, we do not want God in our lives, so why do we pretend to be a spiritual nation? Politically we want to remove every vestige of God from America, but when a tragedy such has Hurricane Katrina threatens us, the public official makes a plea, "Pray to God that this hurricane does not hit us." So in America, it's OK to pray publicly when an impending disaster looms, but otherwise, it's unacceptable. We just can't have it both ways. Either we claim to be a God-fearing nation or we're not. But let's ask ourselves these questions: Where is the Christian Church in all of this? Why are their voices not overpowering those of the atheists, skeptics, and liberal left that seem to be yelling the loudest?

In his anti-Christian manifesto, *Letter to a Christian Nation*, self-acclaimed atheist Sam Harris states, "I have set out to demolish the intellectual and moral pretensions of Christianity in its most committed forms." Part of his argumentative platform is that the Christians of today are simply pointing fingers but not combating the looming threat of radical Islam.[3] Perhaps Harris has a valid point. If Christians sit idle and allow the tyranny of radical Islam to rule, then they deserve what they get. But then again, where were the members of our Christian nation when a federal judge ruled in 2002 that the monument of the Ten Commandments be removed from Alabama Chief Justice Roy Moore's courtroom claiming that it violated the constitution's ban on government promotion of religion? When a member of the *clergy* states, "This [removal of the Ten Commandments] is a tremendous victory for the rule of law and respect for religious diversity,"[4] where does that leave the layman in the street? If this were an infraction against Islam, there would have been such a violent outpouring by Muslims—rage if you will—that the lawmakers would have caved in and yielded to their demands. So why were the Christians such a mute force? Because they are not vigilant of the erosion of spiritual values and lack the conviction to act.

It was on June 14, 1954, that President Dwight D. Eisenhower added the phrase "Under God" to the Pledge of Allegiance. He stated, "In this way we are reaffirming the transcendence of religious faith in America's heritage and future, in this way we shall constantly strengthen those spiritual weapons which forever will be our country's most powerful resource in peace and war."[5] We must recognize that it is incumbent upon us to understand President Eisenhower's use of the phrase, "strengthen those spiritual weapons that will be our most powerful resource in peace and war," in a time when America is being strangled by the unceasing threat of Islamic terrorists determined to destroy us. On September 14, 2005, a federal judge in San Francisco declared the reciting of the Pledge of Allegiance in public schools unconstitutional. U. S. District Judge Lawrence Karlton ruled that the pledge's reference to one nation "under God" violates school children's right to be "free from a coercive requirement to affirm God."[6] Prior to this event, the Alabama Court of Appeals (11th Court) in 1985 ruled against one-minute periods of silence in schools "for meditation or voluntary prayer."[7]

Earlier, on June 25, 1962, thirty-nine million students were forbidden to do what they and their predecessors had been doing since the founding of our nation—publicly calling upon the name of the Lord at the beginning of each school day. Citing David Barton, Gary Bergel adds:

> The New York school children which prompted the Engel vs. Vitale ruling had simply prayed: "Almighty God, we acknowledge our dependence on Thee and

beg Thy blessing over us, our parents, our teachers and our nation." America has experienced radical decline in each of the four areas which the children's prayer touched upon: youth, family, education, national life. The removal of prayer from our schools was a violation of the Third commandment which commands us "not to take the name of the Lord in vain." By the judicial act of forbidding invocation, the Court audaciously elevated a secularized system of education beyond the authority, reach and blessing of God Himself. Worse than taking the Lord's sacred name in vain is treating it with contempt, denying it rightful place and stripping it from public use and even from the lips of children.

Think then, what happens to a nation rife with perjury, broken marriage covenants, unforgiveness, cult with demonic covenants, extortion, bribery, libel, slander, profanity, hypocrisy, idle talk, and lawsuits initiated solely for revenge and personal gain. We are living witnesses that truly, "the Lord does not hold such a nation guiltless."[8]

Removing God from the pledge and prayer from public schools was only one of the many tactics being used by anti-God forces to subvert our nation's value system. Robert W. Lee argues that public schools have abandoned religious values in favor of secular humanism, inculcating children with dangerous messages that promote promiscuity, drug use, and a lack of respect for life. Lee contends that students are being enticed to discard values and religious beliefs of their families and create their own sets of values.[9] Many youngsters have been encouraged by values clarification to reject the traditional Judeo-Christian prohibition against sexual perversion and adopt an open and assertive homosexual lifestyle. The "Children of the Rainbow" curriculum, supported by the open lesbian Deborah Glick, former Assembly-woman of New York, sought to indoctrinate children in the homosexual lifestyle through the gay rights ideology by saturating classroom subjects with their pro-homosexual messages.[10] The statement that Americans have given so far to God and our nation is: Remove prayer and every vestige of the God of our founding fathers from our land and replace Him with Allah. Praying to Allah is OK. Then, remove the values systems from our Judeo-Christian base and replace it with a subverted one that includes a version of our belief system.

In December of 2005, U. S. District Judge John E. Jones of Harrisburg, Pa., announced a stinging attack on the Dover Area School Board saying that its science curriculum that included Intelligent Design violated the constitutional separation of church and state. He argued that Intelligent Design is the concept of Creationism in disguise.[11] Adding this to the list then, we have arrived at a place where we have removed the God of the Bible from the pledge and prayer in school and replaced Him with Allah. Then we removed Creationism and replaced it with Evolutionism. So, is it any wonder that we have the largest amount of school shootings in the world? Where school districts have to maintain high security with guards and metal detectors? Yes, we have succeeded in removing the Bible and replacing it with weapons. These weapons are not only firearms, but weapons determined to undermine one of the basic foundations of our nation, the family.

The Awakened American Family

> **MORAL BANKRUPTCY**
> The moral bankruptcy of America over the past thirty years has been our national shame. It has made us a disgrace in the eyes of the world. We know now that the anger and bitterness of Muslim nations toward this country derives in large part from this grinding down of morality and culture through the media, the movies, and the lifestyles popularized by global forums such as MTV. No one, or course, defends the use of terror of any kind to execute moral judgment; but we cannot help but see that America's loss of modesty and self-restraint has provoked outrage and resentment around the world. –Jim Nelson Black, *Loss of Faith in America*. Excerpt from *America, Return to God*.

When Biblical Natural Law was rejected in 1962, the educational SAT total scores dropped sharply while morality, namely sexually transmitted disease in youth, increased dramatically.[12] Additionally, violent behavior has risen at a staggering rate since the landmark decision in 1962 as well. This "moral awakening" in America has had a seriously damaging effect on the family since 1962, where the stability of the American family has suffered incalculable damage when the single parent of the household is a female and no spouse is present.[13]

The rebellious spirit of the Enlightenment that befell Europe has mutated into a "Moral Awakening" of debauchery here in America. This radical liberation mindset that sought freedom from rules of every kind now spends its days in search of new highs in sex, drugs, and acid rock and roll. In short, this amounts to an awakened family that has rejected God. Our awakened American family has scoffed at the Judeo-Christian heritage, and then filled the void with metaphysical cults, yoga, Chinese I Ching, Zen, and Tibetan Buddhism. If that weren't bad enough, let's throw in the worship of the earth goddess, Gaea. In addition to the hallmark celebration of vulgarity in the music industry and popular media, children are now assaulted at home with bathroom humor cartoons with characters expelling gas and making obscene gestures without a peep of complaint from their parents.

The price tag on America's sexual freedom seems to be limitless. Today more than sixty-five million Americans are infected with sexually transmitted diseases (STDs). Many of these diseases have no known cures. In Drs. Lawrence J. and Brian F. McNamee's book, *AIDS, The Nation's First Politically Protected Disease*, they furnish the general public with the ominous financial burden of AIDS patients to American Health Insurance companies: "...the direct medical costs alone could be nearly $1 trillion annually in today's money—an expenditure that is clearly impossible."[14] Clearly our nation has chosen sodomy over sanity where the secular world would rather finance homosexuality than stand up against the humanist world view that teaches we should abdicate our responsibility of protecting the sanctity of the family before God.

The American family has surely been awakened, only to find two enemies seeking to destroy it: the Muslim threat and the homosexual agenda. "There is no more ominous threat to our future as a nation than the campaign for homosexuality being waged today in the popular media. The same perversions that brought ancient societies to ruin—and that have been anathema to every civilization known to man for more than five thousand years—are now paraded in the public eye and almost universally defended as inalienable rights. We find that forty-five percent of adults in this country believe homosexuality is an "acceptable lifestyle," and thanks to relentless programming in the schools, eighty-five percent of high school seniors say homosexuality is acceptable. Likewise, eighty-six percent say that homosexuality is determined at birth."[15] Every age and nation has its moral issues that define it, and history will look back on America and say that its greatness, with its valiant patriarchs and noble countrymen who dictated allegiance to God, was overcome with pride and liberty that led it to spiral down into depravity.

God has chosen three areas of jurisdiction in which to govern mankind: the Government, the Church, and the Family. The "sexually awakened America" has posed the greatest threat to all of these institutions. When the nation's highest officer, the President, can publicly lie to over 250 million Americans and say "he did not have sex" with one of his interns, and when a pastor-leader in a large Baptist denomination can be embroiled in homosexuality, then what can we expect to occur in the family? What we can expect is rapidly becoming a reality. The family is being dismantled before our very eyes. According to a recent Barna Poll:

ON SEXUALITY:
Perhaps no moral dimension has changed as much as Americans' perspective and behaviors related to sexuality. Among the 32 factors examined in the research, eight of them related to such topics as extramarital sex, pornography, homosexuality, and sexual fantasies. In all eight of these areas, Busters (American's in their twenties and thirties), were significantly different from older Americans. Busters were twice as likely to have viewed sexually explicit movies or videos; two and a half times more likely to report having had a sexual encounter outside of marriage; and three times more likely to have viewed sexually graphic content online. More than two-thirds of the generation said that cohabitation and sexual fantasies are morally acceptable behaviors, compared with half of older adults. Most young adults contended that engaging in sex outside of marriage and viewing pornography are not morally problematic, while only one-third of pre-Busters agreed. Almost half of Busters believed that sexual relationships between people of the same sex are acceptable, compared with one-quarter of older adults. Young adults were significantly more likely to accept gambling, profanity, intoxication, and

illegal drug use as morally acceptable behaviors. Busters' perspectives were no different from that of their elders on three issues: the acceptability of abortion, allowing the "f-word" on broadcast television, and deeming divorce not to be a sin.

BARNA WRITES ON OTHER MATTERS:
Nearly half of all pre-Busters said they view moral truth as absolute, but only three out of 10 Busters embraced the concept of absolute truth. Two-thirds of those over 40 said humans should determine what is right and wrong morally by examining God's principles; less than half of Busters felt this way. Instead, nearly half of Busters said that ethics and morals are based on "what is right for the person," compared with just one-quarter of pre-Busters.

We expect to see this mindset of sexual entitlement translate into increased appetites for pornography, unfiltered acceptance of sexual themes and content in media, and continued dissolution of marriages due to infidelity. It seems entirely possible that current events such as the Mark Foley scandal, instances of abuse by clergy, and the sexually oriented school shootings of recent months are not mere aberrations, but symptoms of a sexually unrestrained society.[16]

The question that begs to be answered is, why do the "Busters" of today set the standards? Where is the Church in all of this? Why isn't the Church setting the standard instead

of the secular world?
Could it be that the Church is sleeping?

Filling the Spiritual Vacuum

The unrelenting attack on America's Judeo-Christian heritage has left a vacuous chasm that is being filled by other religions. With Christianity being purged from the public arena a new civil religion is emerging to take its place. Gene Edward Veith wrote:

> Now, however, the distinctly Christian elements that have made their way into America's civil religion—such as monuments of the Ten Commandments in courthouses—are being purged away with inquisitorial zeal. The reasons given are not so much those of secularism, that religion has no place in the public square, but of religious diversity. It is not fair, say the Commandment removers, to privilege Christianity. What about Muslims, Hindus, pagans, and people with self-made theologies? Legislatures still open with a prayer, but now it may be delivered by a Muslim imam or a Buddhist monk rather than by a Christian clergyman. Prisons now hire chaplains who are not only Muslims but radical jihadists recruiting for terrorism. Wisconsin has hired the Rev. Jamyi Witch, a member of the neo-pagan sect of Wicca, as a prison chaplain.
>
> This was the approach of ancient Rome, which simply added the gods of the lands they conquered

to their Pantheon. Rome was religiously inclusive, working all of the cultural religions into a single civil religion, and it was famously tolerant. Its tolerance ended when it came to Christianity, which condemned the other gods as idols and insisted that Christ is the only way to salvation. Christians refused to burn the incense to the civil religion and many paid for their "intolerance" with their lives.[17]

With America's civil religion becoming polytheistic, Christians may have to bow to these gods or bow out of society.

Consider this troublesome fact: King Abdullah of Saudi Arabia and his relatives since 1975 have financed more than $70 billion in building mosques and Islamic centers worldwide, including more than $300 million in the Unites States, where most Muslims studying in Arabic use Saudi textbooks, some of which are violently anti-Christian and anti-Jewish.[18] Many of these mosques teach the tencts of radical Wahhabism that is bent on overthrowing Western democracy. With this specter in mind, is it any wonder that a seventy-three-year-old German pastor, Rev. Roland Weisselberg, soaked himself in gasoline and set himself on fire in fear that Christian Europe would be overwhelmed by Islam?[19] Will American pastors also rise to the challenge to fill the void being rapidly occupied by Eastern religions?

Maybe.

Eastern religions are not the only threat to America. In 1973, Americans spent about $10 million on pornography. By 1987 that figure had grown to more than $8 billion.

Today, by some estimates, the figure exceeds $14 billion. Pornography is considered by many in the investment community to be the new glamour stock of the 21st century.[20] And we haven't even looked at the impact the Roe vs. Wade Supreme Court ruling of 1973 has had on the American family. It is estimated that since the inception of the ruling, there have been over forty-one million abortions performed in America, of which late-term abortions and partial-birth abortions are no longer rare. Francis Schaeffer called the abortion catastrophe the "American Holocaust," comparing it to the Nazi holocaust where six million Jews were slaughtered. We have outnumbered the Nazi war machine and paid for it with tax dollars. Schaeffer added ,". . . that parents who are apprehended for child abuse must feel that the system is somewhat unfair in that they can be arrested for beating their child, whereas people who kill their infant before birth go scot free—in fact have society's approval." It was Mother Teresa who said, "If a mother can kill her own children, then what can be next?" Good question. Here's what came next:

1. North Lauderdale, FL (Feb. 11, 2005). *Mother Who Tossed Newborn From Car Traced.* The boy, believed to be less than an hour old, was thrown out of a car alongside a busy street Thursday afternoon, police said. The eight-pound, two-ounce boy, whose umbilical cord was still attached, survived with minor injuries and was hospitalized in good condition Friday. Nurses at the hospital have nicknamed the child Johnny. –aolsvc.news.com

2. Tyler, TX (May, 2003). *Verdict of Insanity.* Deanna Laney, thirty-nine, is declared not guilty by reason of insanity after bashing to death with rocks her two sons she had home schooled, Joshua, eight, and Luke, six, in the front yard in the middle of the night. *World Magazine.*

3. Houston, TX (June 20, 2001). Rusty Yates received a startling call from his wife, Andrea, whom he had left only an hour before going to work. When he arrived at home, he found on a double bed in a back master bedroom he found his four children laid out beneath a sheet, clothed and soaking wet. All of them were dead, with their eyes wide open. In the bathtub, submerged amid feces and vomit floating on the surface was his oldest, and he was also dead. The mother, Andrea, led the police officers to the children and told them without emotion that she had killed her children. She looked dispassionately at the gathering crowd of curious neighbors as she got into the police car.

www.crimelibrary.com

4. Virginia (2000). Elizabeth Renee Otte is sentenced to five years in prison for killing her month-old son in microwave oven back in 1999.

www.crimelibrary.com

5. Union, SC (Oct. 25, 1994). Susan Smith, fearful that her married lover would reject her with her two children, Michael, age three, and Alex, age fourteen months, drove her car to a gravel boat ramp then got out of the car, released the emergency

brake, and watched the car roll into the canal. Smith watched as the car floated and filled with water. Finally it went under and she ran to a nearby house, screaming that a black man
had accosted her at a traffic light and taken her car with her sons inside. It wasn't long before investigators figured out what she had done, found the car, and brought the two small bodies out of the water. Smith was convicted of murder and is serving a life sentence in prison.

America has been awakened, but the awakening has brought us lower than low. Nature itself has shown that in the animal kingdom they don't kill their young, but society has placed a higher value on animals than on humans. The snail darter, the sea turtle, and the manatee are protected—where fines and imprisonment are meted out if their breeding grounds or nests are disturbed, but killing children by aborting them is legal. America is descending down the abyss into depravity when animal rights eclipse those of humans. In an article called, "The Madness of the Animal-Rights Movement" by David Kupelian of WorldNetDaily.com he recounts an horrific story out of Scotland. Social workers were called to rescue a pet monkey from the filthy, drug-infested apartment of a couple of heroin addicts. Contacting an animal-welfare group, the social workers took great pains to make sure the animal was removed from the squalid cesspool of a home. But the social workers neglected to do anything about the little girl living with the couple. The five-year old's fingernails had not been cut for more than a year, she was covered with bed sores, lying in human waste, and wearing a plaster cast on her broken leg that should have been removed ten months earlier. When doctors eventually removed the cast from the girl, whose leg was permanently scarred, they found spoons, a fork, and a pen she had used to try to scratch her ulcers. A judge rebuked the social workers, noting incredulously that they had visited the couple's house eighteen times and had gone inside four times, but failed to take note of or do anything about the poor girl's plight. Absurd you say? Yes, we have placed animal life above human life. More proof:

The organization, PETA (People for the Ethical Treatment of Animals) is the largest animal-rights organization on the planet, bragging of 600,000 members. "To demonstrate its corporate citizenship in promoting alternative methods of testing, PETA has made grants totaling $300,000 to two research firms 'to assist in the validation of non-animal test methods to replace existing animal tests.'" What sort of non-animal testing? How about human embryos? Human babies, you see, are not as important as rats.

Kupelian also noted in his article that the Rev. Msgr. Dennis N. Schnurr accused the National Institutes of Health of the charge that their new guidelines that place human embryos outside the womb for exploitation and destruction are treating human life as nothing more than "tissue." He added that, ". . . the human embryo effectively ranks lower in status than a laboratory animal." Kupelian summarized his findings by saying, "The real message of the radical animal rights movement is that people are only animals. . .

so we act like animals, we do what animals do. They eat each other, mate in the street, run around naked—kind of like the '60s again, with 'sex, drugs and rock and roll.'" Citing Steven Segal, one of PETA's celebrity advocates who said, "We have to view all life as equal," Kupelian remarked in response, "[this] is a round-about way of saying that human beings are no more than animals and therefore have no souls."[21]

After this testimony, we as Americans have the audacity to ask, "Where was God on 9/11?"

The Wrath of Abandonment

Divine principles cannot be modified or revoked. An old aphorism states, "Be careful what you wish or pray for." We live in an age where America has asked and worked toward being enlightened and awakened in every sense of the word, and yes, God has been gracious and allowed it. But that request came at a great price, for the psalmist warned against such a petition if it led to treachery when the nation making the appeal flouts its sin in His face. The warning came in Psalm 106:15: "So he gave them what they asked for, but sent *leanness* to their souls" (KJV, emphasis added).

That leanness has come to America in the form of abandonment.

Abandonment is a punitive measure of divine wrath that the apostle Paul explains in Romans 1. "It is a frightening reality. God gives people over completely to their own sinful desires, steps back, and lets them go. They want their sin, so God allows them to have it without hindrance. He simply withdraws the blessing of His restraining grace."[22]

This was the fate of King Rehoboam, the first king of

Judah at the beginning of the divided kingdom period. After his position as king was established and he had become strong, he led Israel to abandon the law of the Lord. In turn, the Egyptian king Shishak attacked Jerusalem during the fifth year of his reign. God sent the prophet Shemaiah to Rehoboam and said, "This is what the LORD says, 'You have abandoned me; therefore I now abandon you to Shishak'" (2 Chronicles 12:5).

Rehoboam, fearful of divine wrath as the consequence of his disobedience, humbled himself and repented. Accordingly, the Lord reduced his punishment. Instead of allowing Shishak to totally destroy Jerusalem, God said, "...You will become subject to him, so that [you] may learn the difference between serving me and serving the kings of other lands," (2 Chronicles 12:8). God then allowed Shishak king of Egypt to strip down and carry off all the national treasures of Solomon's temple and the kings' palace.

This, dear reader, is exactly what is happening to America since we have abandoned God. God is allowing our national treasury to be systematically transferred to the oil-rich Arab countries and us to spend trillions of dollars in defense of America's borders from terrorist regimes.

This is God's measure of abandonment on America.

CHAPTER 2
Sleepwalking America

Make the heart of this people calloused; make their ears dull and close their eyes. Otherwise they might see with their eyes, hear with their ears, understand with their hearts, and turn and be healed . . . For this people's heart has become calloused; they hardly hear with their ears, and they have closed their eyes. . . . For the LORD hath poured out upon you the spirit of deep sleep, and hath closed your eyes: the prophets and your rulers, the seers hath he covered. –The Prophet Isaiah 6:10; 29:10; the Apostle Matthew 13:15 (NIV)

The people of America have spoken: We do not want God ruling over us. We want every vestige of God removed from our sight. The people have shouted, "We want a democracy, not a theocracy!" Thus, God has granted our request and therefore America has come under the curse of abandonment where our hearts have become calloused, our ears dull, and our eyes closed—we have fallen into a deep spiritual sleep. *We're not really walking, but sleepwalking!* The historical outcome of a people who have taken this position is the gradual erosion of spiritual, ethical and moral values. This is not a new phenomenon. This condition befell the nation of Israel during the time of Samuel the Judge. The people compared their theocratic government, worship of God, and holy lifestyle to their neighboring heathen nations and saw the so-called freedom, and then began to criticize and find fault with their religious leaders. Before long, they formed a committee and came to Samuel and stated, ". . . appoint a king to lead us, such as all the other nations have" (I Samuel 8:5). Samuel was very grieved and prayed to the Lord who answered him: "Listen to all that the people are saying to you; it is not you they have rejected, *but they have rejected me as their king* . . .forsaking me and serving other gods . . . but warn them solemnly and let them know what the king who will reign over them will do" (I Samuel 8:7-9, emphasis added).

Samuel rehearsed these words in the ears of the leaders and reminded them that earthly kings exact payment for their services, and they would be in servitude. The king will make slaves of your children, your children will serve him in wars, your property will be taxed and seized by the government, and then you will cry out for relief from him whom you have chosen—but the Lord will not answer you in that day. Despite the warning, the nation replied, "No, we want a king over us so we will be like all the other nations" (I Samuel 8:18-19). This was the beginning of their undoing since their demand for a king was tantamount to asking for a pagan god to rule over them which God had condemned in Levitical law (Lev. 20:23). Their request would, therefore, come at a great price. Their choice, Saul, nearly brought the kingdom to ruin until God raised up His choice for a king, David, the son of Jesse.

America has cavorted with the gods of humanism, materialism, narcissism, hedonism, existentialism, pluralism, paganism, and atheism. We have given honor to Satan; now the time has come for Moloch to exact his sacrifice of blood. As a nation we have become catatonic and desensitized—totally insensible to sin and its consequences. And it will be shown that this terrible price we are paying is due to the negligence and irresponsibility of the sleepwalking Church.

To demonstrate this price, namely, insensibility to spiritual principles and the resultant action taken to avoid sin, a Barna study taken five years after 9/11 revealed some harrowing statistics:

> 1. Despite an intense surge in religious activity and expression in the weeks immediately following 9/11, the faith of Americans is virtually indistinguishable today compared to pre-attack conditions. In other words, using nineteen different dimensions of spirituality and beliefs, remarkably, none of those nineteen indicators are statistically different from the summer before the attacks.
>
> 2. The research explored three areas of religious activity, five indicators of religious belief, three pertaining to spiritual commitment, and eight related

to faith identity. The most recent measurements for all of those indicators of faith are virtually identical to the norms prior to September 11, 2001.

3. In the immediate aftermath of the attacks, half of all Americans said their faith helped them cope with the shock and uncertainty. The change most widely reported was a significant spike in church attendance, with some churches experiencing more than double their normal crowd on the Sunday after the shocking event. However, by the time January 2002 rolled around, churchgoing was back to pre-attack levels, and has remained consistent in the five years since.

4. As of October, 2001, American's engagement in Bible reading and prayer was no different than pre-attack levels and has been essentially consistent from that point on.

5. Throughout the period of emotional insecurity, many adults became increasingly skeptical of traditional religious views.

6. As of the summer of 2006, the five religious beliefs that were assessed in the research—beliefs about the devil, salvation, the nature of God, responsibility to evangelize, and the accuracy of the Bible's teachings—were indistinguishable from the profile of spiritual beliefs back in the summer of 2001. [23]

Analyzing these findings leads the author to believe that not only is America sleepwalking, but the Church is also sleepwalking. If indeed the Church is sleepwalking, then we can expect little impact inside the Church and little impact from the Church to affect change in the outside world. The director of the Barna study, David Kinnaman, summarized the study of the post-9/11 attacks this way:

> Many Christian leaders predicted that terrorism on U. S. soil would catalyze a spiritual awakening in the country. The first few weeks were promising. But people quickly returned to their standard, faith-as-usual lives: within a month, most of their spiritual fervor was gone. Within 90 days, surprisingly few people were pursuing important questions about faith and spirituality. Now, five years removed from that fateful day, spiritually speaking, it's as if nothing significant ever happened. People used faith like a giant band-aid—it helped people deal with the ugliness of the event but it offered little in the way of deep healing and it was discarded after a brief period of use.[24]

In the mind of God, nothing has changed. Both the nation and the Church are sleepwalking.

Our Founding Fathers Are Turning In Their Graves

While the nation and the Church sleepwalk, the enemies from without and within conspire to overthrow the very basic religious and democratic freedoms our founding fathers fought so hard to create and protect. Should they return today, they would be ashamed at the way their fellow

Dr. Ralph D. Curtin

Americans and the modern Church have dismantled the precepts and tenets they were convinced to be the foundation of our nation's heritage. Doubtless, now they must be turning in their graves at the way we have treated their God whom they believed granted them possession of this glorious land. They believed that the Sovereign God of the Bible must be honored in order for our nation to be blessed and prosper. Here is a sampling of their convictions:

- William Penn (1644-1718): "If we are not ruled by God we will be ruled by tyrants."
- Noah Webster (1758-1843): "The moral principles and precepts contained in the scriptures ought to form the basis of all our civil constitutions and laws ... All the miseries and evils which men suffer, from vice, crime, ambition, injustice, oppression, slavery, and war, proceed from their despairing or neglecting the precepts contained in the Bible."
- James Madison (1751-1836): "We have staked the whole future of American civilization, not upon the power of government, far from it. We have staked the future of all of our Institutions upon the capacity of mankind for self-government, upon the capacity of each and all of us to govern ourselves, to control our selves, to sustain ourselves according to the Ten Commandments of God ..."
- Samuel Adams (1722-1803): "We have this day restored the Sovereign to Whom all men ought to be obedient. He reigns in heaven and from the rising of the sun, let His Kingdom

come."

- Robert E. Lee (1807-1870): "Knowing that intercessory prayer is our mightiest weapon and that the supreme call for all Christians today, I pleadingly urge our people everywhere to pray. Believing that prayer is the greatest contribution our people can make in this critical hour, I humbly urge that we take time to pray—to really pray."

Thomas Jefferson, the third president of the United States, was severely distressed over the sin that he saw in our nation. He wrote: "I tremble for my country when I reflect that God is just." Our founding fathers embraced individual freedom, but not at the cost of a permissive lifestyle that does not fear God and rejects restraint. The Church too, has culpability since it has failed in its efforts to restrain the rise of evil and moral compromise in America.

> *n* to God.
>
> *od.* **GEJECTED**
> I wrote for them the many things of my law, but

The enemies of our nation from without may be radical Islamic terrorists, but we face an even greater enemy from within. They are those treasonous factions determined to undermine the founding father's beliefs and principles. The constant supplanting of these beliefs and principles is prohibiting America from distinguishing the difference between the holy and the profane. United we stand, divided we fall is the proclamation of our founding fathers—a principle we seem doomed to violate. America is divided between the liberal left and the conservative right, and the gulf is widening dramatically due to internal corruption. If Abraham Lincoln were alive, things might be quite different for his belief was to do what was necessary to protect the nation he loved from collapsing from within:

> Lincoln suspended the writ of *habeas corpus* during the Civil War, and had civilians in the South tried by military tribunals without the use of either a jury or the normal rules of evidence, and made use of wholesale internment of individuals suspected of supporting the Confederacy—and yet the Supreme Court was silent. Lincoln was forced to assume extraordinary powers when the security of the American nation was in jeopardy. Among his other encroachments on civil liberties which he deemed to be endangering the United States, he authorized the execution by firing squad of *those who used their freedom of speech to demoralize the Union armies and incite criminal defections* (emphasis added).[25]

Sleepwalking America and the sleepwalking Church has allowed the liberal left to sabotage and demoralize its citizens and our Judeo-Christian way of life by systematically dismantling The Constitution and subverting the very laws of our land by relentless acts of subterfuge. These treasonous acts are disguised as "rights."

Distinction Between Liberty And License

Sleepwalking America has allowed subversive groups such as the ACLU to systematically disassemble the founding fathers' interpretation of Holy Writ and its application to society so that we cannot differentiate between what is liberty and what is license. One of America's patriarch's, John Adams (1735-1826), believed we should not cross that barrier for fear that the concept of law and government would be jeopardized. Concerning John Adams, Terry Eastland wrote:

> ...most people agreed that our law was rooted, as John Adams had said, in a common moral and religious tradition, one that stretched back to the time Moses went up to Mount Sinai. Similarly almost everyone agreed that our liberties were God-given and should be exercised responsibly. *There was a distinction between liberty and license* (emphasis added).[26]

Today, that distinction is referred in today's colloquial language as a "gray area." And it's in this "gray area" that we find ourselves currently. We are unable to label adultery, homosexuality, pedophilia, pornography, and incest "sin" because it may "offend" some group or association—never giving thought to the offense our sin is before God. Those that are "offended" cry foul under the heading of "rights."

The chief advocate for "rights" in America today is the ACLU, an organization founded by Roger Baldwin in 1920 with strong leanings toward Communism and a staunch liberal.[27] This same "un-American" was awarded in 1981 the highest civilian honor our country offers, the Medal of Freedom, by then President Jimmy Carter.[28]

From its inception, the ACLU has only one agenda: to destroy from within America's Judeo-Christian heritage by attacking the very undercarriage that our founding fathers labored so strenuously to build. The scheme comes under the guise of "rights" or "liberty." Unfortunately, Baldwin's ideology is still employed by the ACLU today as it promotes an anarchical philosophy where one can do virtually anything and no one individual, no religion or its God, and no government entity has the authority or power to stop them. Baldwin's neo-Nazi platform for the goals and objectives of the ACLU were clearly defined by him in his thirtieth-anniversary Harvard University class book: "I am for Socialism, disarmament, and ultimately the abolishing of the state itself as an instrument of violence and compulsion. I seek social ownership of property, the abolition of the propertied class, and sole control by those who produce wealth. Communism is the goal."[29]

The ACLU, America's religious antagonist, has an enormous war chest in which to wage battle, almost uncontested, against any adversary that declares itself to be Christian in America. Under the banner of "liberty" and "rights," the ACLU has deceived the public into thinking they are being protected from the government or from an organized religion that may be attempting to strip them of their rights. William Donohue wrote, "By wrapping themselves in the flag, then, civil libertarians could pursue their political objectives while feigning loyalty to the nation."[30]

In actuality:

> The ACLU is *against* the freedom of parents to pass their faith and values along to their children. It is *against* the freedom of organizations such as the Boy Scouts to set standard rules of conduct for their leaders. It is *against* the freedom of churches to publicly teach and proclaim the uncensored Word of God in the public square. It is *against* many of the freedoms and our nation's sovereignty that our forefathers fought and died for in the American Revolution and the many wars that followed ... The ACLU's goal is a secularized "tolerant" America where religious speech is not only silenced but punished; where unwanted human life is quickly and easily discarded, hopefully at taxpayer expense; where the God-ordained institution of marriage and the family is on its way to becoming a distant memory, and where their "tolerance" is the silence of many others (emphasis added).[31]

In the year 1920, a joint committee of New York State Legislature declared the ACLU as a "supporter of all subversive movements, and its propaganda is detrimental to the interests of the state. The ACLU attempts not only to protect crime, but to encourage attacks upon our institutions in every form."[32] My question is, where was the Church in all of this? How could the Church have allowed the ACLU to gain such momentum over the years and become the monster it now is? In a later chapter it will be demonstrated that the Church has great culpability in permitting the emasculation of the Constitution and the outworking of such an atrocity in American history.

Mutilating The First Amendment

The design of the First Amendment of the Constitution regarding religion was only that the federal government was to be prohibited from establishing a national church, not the censoring of public religious practice or expression.[33] The ACLU and its henchmen have relentlessly attacked faith-based organizations with distorted interpretations of the First Amendment in collusion with liberal court Justices. "Courts that at once dared not violate the laws of God—and enforced rules against blasphemy—now openly mock His name . . . The First Amendment was never intended to protect obscene material. Obscenity is outside the scope of the First Amendment and is not considered to be 'speech' as defined in the Constitution. In fact, the First Amendment calls for self-restraint and for individuals to be held responsible for their actions."[34]

The mutilation of the First Amendment has given license to the ACLU through victories in the courtroom to pander for the pornographer, to act as the purveyor for the pedophile, and the procurer for the profligate—the end game being that "rights" eclipse personal responsibility—the solution for sinful behavior commanded by God. The "promotion of 'individual rights' ultimately results in a society in which the rights of individuals drastically outweigh the collective responsibility individuals should have to society or the concept of a higher law or duty individuals are responsible to follow."35

The ACLU has left its black mark on enough of America so that it would be unrecognizable and utterly abhorrent to the men who first framed the Constitution. The ACLU's "accomplishments" are a stench in the nostrils of the God that granted the Pilgrims their landing on Plymouth Rock in 1620. The ACLU's legacy is penned in blood for its contribution to the abortion-rights movement, its adverse effect on the one-man, one-woman marriage; its disdain for the authoritative role of parents, its abhorrence of the Boy Scouts, and its diligence in the undermining of the Judeo-Christian heritage in America. Kudos! But remember this somber warning: God will not be mocked.

The Fruit Of Abused Liberty And License

Cincinnati, Ohio—"A prosecutor said on Saturday he was appalled by an appeals court decision to overturn a prison sentence for a child rapist because the judge when imposing punishment had quoted from the Bible. In a 2-1 verdict, the Ohio First District Court of Appeals reversed the 51-year sentence of James Arnett, 33, who had pleaded guilty in January 1998 to 10 counts of rape involving the 8-year-old daughter of his fiancé."36 This is the kind of treatment we can expect for criminals when the mindset of the ACLU is let loose in the courts thereby distorting both liberty and license. It gets worse.

Richmond, Virginia— A witch holding to Wiccan, who was barred from saying a prayer to open board of supervisors meetings was exonerated by U. S. District Court Judge Dennis W. Dohnal who said, "Pagans can pray, too." The judge claimed discrimination against Cyndi Simpson when it [the board] prohibited her from joining a list of clergy who deliver the invocations. Simpson was quoted as saying, "it [the decision] would bring credibility to witchcraft as a religion." Kent Willis, executive director of the ACLU who filed the lawsuit, "called the ruling a victory for non-majority religions."[37]

Iowa—A judge has ruled that a Bible-based prison program violates the First Amendment's freedom of religion clause by using state funds to promote Christianity to inmates, but it is a known fact that Saudi-based Wahhabism proselytizing programs directed toward American's prison population with the purpose of converting American prisoners to Islam is constantly on the rise.[38]

The question that must be answered is: Why doesn't the ACLU go after the radical Wahhabis operating here in the United States? Could it be that they are fearful that radical Islam would violently react and they would then be branded as being anti-Islamic? Intolerant? But being anti-Christian is OK. Something is wrong in our nation when Americans and the Church body can sit back wearing blindfolds and allow this kind of prejudice to prosper, knowing that this subversive organization is dedicated to the spiritual, moral, and ethical collapse of our nation.

Recipe For Disaster
From a Communist Rules for Revolution document captured by Allied Forces in Europe after WWI in 1919:

1. Corrupt the young; get them away from religion. Get them interested in sex. Make them superficial; destroy their toughness.

2. Control the media, all means of communications and publicity.

3. Get people's minds off their government. Focusing their attention on athletics, sexy books and trivialities.

4. Divide the people into hostile groups against each other by constantly harping on controversial matters of no importance.

5. Destroy people's faith in their national leaders by holding them up for contempt, ridicule and distrust.

6. Always preach democracy, but seize power as fast and ruthless as possible.

7. Encourage civil disorder and foster a soft and lenient attitude on the part of the government (law and courts) toward such disorders.[39]

America and the corporate Church must recognize the onslaught to our Judeo-Christian heritage that looms on the horizon. The systematic tearing down of our Constitution under the pretense of rights and liberty has given license to the monster from the Id that will soon be unleashed upon the people of Judaism and Christianity that will make the Crusades pale into insignificance. The adverse effect of this attack has already taken its toll on the Church where "Notional Christians" are being produced.

Barna describes Notional Christians "as those who

describe themselves as Christians, but do not believe that they will have eternal life because of their reliance upon the death and resurrection of Jesus Christ and the grace extended to people through a relationship with Christ (a large portion of these individuals believe they will have eternal life, but *not because of a grace-based relationship with Jesus Christ.* Notional Christians represent 39% of the population) (emphasis added)."[40] When "Christians" buy into the lie that salvation can come by any other means than reliance upon the death and resurrection of Jesus Christ, being regenerated in the Spirit, then we as a "Church" have accepted the muddled theology that leads to heresy. This is exactly what Satan and the liberal forces have revved up their engines to achieve. To sleepwalking America and a sleeping Church, the prospect for restoration and revival remains to be only a dream.

CHAPTER 3
The Sleeping Church

Why are you sleeping? Jesus Christ, Luke 22:46

Our first-century Christian fathers would be astounded and gravely disappointed to see how the Church has evolved! In their time they met in the temple courts or in private homes (cf. Acts 2:46), and during the Roman persecution, catacombs and makeshift buildings—often meeting in the open air as they traveled from town to town, proclaiming the Word of God. But today, the mega-church is equipped with on-campus worlds, complete with shops, gyms, and aerobic centers. Many of the churches rival civic centers with their various programs that include martial arts, motorcycle clubs, and sundry "carnival-like" attractions to draw the crowds.

Under the guise of "needing more room" today's churches are moving away from fertile urban and city environments to "greener pastures" in the suburbs where they don't have to deal with the homeless man who may surprise them by showing up for worship service some Sunday morning. Nor do they have to contend with having to step over a drunk or drug addict who is sleeping or dead in the church vestibule. No, the contemporary church seems to be evolving from the spiritual, evangelical, breathing organism God intended it to be to a secular business that makes people feel good.

The prophets of the Bible would shout a hearty collective "amen!" to the oracles heralded by eighteenth-century Church fathers who proclaimed: "Ought I not to do what I can for the Lord Jesus while He tarries, and *to rouse a slumbering church*" (emphasis added), [41] and to Rev. T. DeWitt Talmage, D. D. who cried out, "O you dead churches, wake up! O Christ, descend!"[42] If *they* believed the Church was slumbering *then*, can you imagine what they would say if they observed today's church!? Either they would declare the church to be sound asleep, or downright dead. What we see happening in the Church is a result of what we see happening in the pew. Indeed, the root cause for the sleeping church is the *sleeping Christian*. But as we will discover, the sleeping Christian is not the only one to blame.

More than a decade has passed since Barna conducted a survey in which he defined a "Christian." His findings help us to recognize the problem that has grown exponentially since the survey was taken:

> While four out of five Americans claim to be "Christian," that word has been made into a generic term referring to someone who is religious, believes in a

universal force of some type or is simply a good person. We think of ourselves as "religious," even though half of us do not engage in consistent religious practices.[43]

The "Christian" of today is often indistinguishable from the non-believer because the Church has lowered the standard of God's righteousness and holiness in order to attract the secular world. A "true Christian" is one who has been Born Again and regenerated in the Spirit according to John 3:16 and Titus 3:5. What we can expect from one who is regenerated in the Spirit is threefold:

    1. There is a passion for the lost. The new Christian sees the non-Christian in a totally different light once he is regenerated, causing him to truly have a burden to reach the unsaved for Christ. They make it their mission in life.
    2. There is a love for the Word of God. Together with the Spirit of God, the Bible becomes their lifeline to God. The regenerated Christian desires to know God and His ways, making the reading of the Word a priority in life.
    3. There is a change of lifestyle (2 Cor. 5:17). The regenerated Christian is empowered with the Holy Spirit to produce the Fruit of the Spirit that enables one to rid their lives of the things that dishonor the Lord. If one belongs to God, change is expected.

Claiming to be a Christian and being one as defined by the Bible is quite different. It is this very difference that accounts for a great deal of the confusion in the Church today. Many are called ["Christian"], but few are chosen. My belief is that this accounts for the present condition of the Church. There are those who claim to be Christian because of family heritage, a church affiliation, or a "television conversion"—but they have not been truly regenerated in the Spirit.

The Reversal of The Great Commission

What we can expect from the Church that is led by liberal pastors and leaders who are "pseudo-Christians" is a reversal of the Great Commission. In the Old Testament economy, Jehovah instructed the children of Israel to build Him a house. Solomon's Temple was that House. The Temple was intended to act as the meeting place between God and man and to draw from the pagan world those who would see the magnificence of Israel's God and come to see and believe in Him. Such was the account of the Queen of Sheba in I Kings 10: "The report I heard in my own country about your achievements and your wisdom is true. But I did not believe these things until I came and saw with my own eyes" (vv. 6-7). God's plan was for the world to "Come!"

In the Christian church today, the magnet that draws crowds to the church is their social programs, pageants, and activities. This is Old Testament theology—"Come!"

This is the reversal of the Great Commission.

The New Testament Great Commission makes it very clear that the Christian is to be trained in evangelism and then they are to "GO!" [Not "Come"]

Therefore *go* and make disciples of all nations, baptizing them in the name of the Father and of the Son and of the Holy Spirit, and *teachin*g them to obey everything I have commanded you (Matthew 28:19-20; emphasis added).

Obedience to the Great Commission is when the Church leadership teaches or trains their Christians in evangelism and sends them out with a hearty, "GO!" into the workplace, the neighborhoods, their families and then proclaim the Gospel. Together, through their testimony as a sold-out Christian, the non-Christian will be drawn to the Church. That's the way it was in the Church of the first century, and that's the way God intended it to be ever since. This is God's recipe for success. Reversing the Great Commission may fill a building, but the man in the pew is nothing more than a spectator.

Selling Liberal Theology

The reversal of the Great Commission can be traced to the pandering of liberal theology. This selling of liberal theology is the principle cause of the corporate Church's inability to restrain and retard the proliferation of sin in the world. Liberal theology preached by liberal pastors and church leaders is the worst kind of heresy. They are not only allowing it, but they are preaching it as well. Gene Edward Veith observes:

> Clint Rainey, a journalism student interning at *The Dallas Morning News*, is put off by the "seeker-

friendly" approach to church that—he contends—does a good job filling up massive church buildings but leaves many empty. Mr. Rainey finds the new churches too materialistic and "impersonal" in every way. He points out that today, one can go into a church (especially a megachurch) of nearly any denomination—Baptist, Presbyterian, Pentecostal, Wesleyan, Lutheran—and be unable to notice any difference among them. They all are likely to use the same praise songs and contemporary worship style. *The sermons will tend to be about practical biblical tips for successful living, and go light on doctrine and sin.* These companies *purposefully avoid all controversial issues, and doctrinal distinctives,* which would limit their marketshare. . . both liberal theologians and church-growth theologians *downplay historic doctrines*, seeing them as divisive and irrelevant. Since some Christians today *make up their own theology* and practices as they go along, oblivious to the time-tested, battle-tested experiences of the church through the ages, their spirituality can seem shallow or "empty" (emphasis added).[44]

As long as we avoid the topic of biblical doctrine, sin or contemporary issues, we will attract crowds and fill the churches. But attracting crowds at the expense of truth is a violation of Christ's words: "Everyone on the side of truth listens to me" (John 18:37). Liberal theology leads to denial of absolute truth. When the Church denies or rejects absolute truth, the Church slides down the slippery slope toward apostasy. Chuck Colson writes: "Christian values are in retreat in the West today, primarily, I believe, *because of the church itself*. If Christianity has failed to stem the rising tide of relativism it is because the church in many instances has lost the convicting force of the gospel message" (emphasis added). [45]

The data collected by pollster Barna supports this view when he compiled a list of biblical dogmas that hopefully Christians from every denomination could agree on, but according to his study, however, forty-nine percent of Protestant pastors reject core biblical beliefs. The core biblical tenets included: absolute moral truth based on the Bible; biblical teaching is accurate; Jesus was without sin; Satan literally exists; God is omnipotent and omniscient; salvation is by grace alone; and Christians have a personal responsibility to evangelize. Additionally, only fifty-one percent agree on the doctrine of the Trinity or the Deity of Christ or other important teachings that are elementary for salvation.[46] If the preacher in the pulpit rejects biblical truth, what can we expect from the congregant in the pew? If the Church is simply preaching good sermons and offering helpful programs to soothe the crowds but avoiding theological issues that shape their lives, then the Church is being disobedient to biblical mandates.

Perhaps the source for such liberal theology is to be found elsewhere? In the seminaries?

The former president of Baylor University, Herbert Reynolds, asserted that he represented the true Baptist tradition and that he didn't agree with "fundamentalists" and that "Baptists do not believe in creeds of any kind, that faith is purely inward, and that individuals have 'soul competency' to form their own theology . . . and that faith has nothing to do with objective knowledge . . . and that faculty are not here to engage in religiosity." When the president of a conservative seminary holds to that liberal position, then what can we expect of those students—would-be pastors—who attend? The outworking is voiced in a Barna study that reported that sixty-four percent of "born-again" Americans and forty percent of "evangelical" Americans say there is no such thing as absolute truth. In other words, the Bible itself may not be valid or that Jesus Christ isn't necessarily the only way to God and so forth. Schaeffer affirmed this view back in 1981 when he wrote:

> ...many Christians do not mean what I mean when I say Christianity is true, or Truth. They are Christians and they believe in, let us say, the truth of creation, the truth of the virgin birth, the truth of Christ's miracles, Christ's substitutionary death, and His coming again. But they stop there with these and other individual truths.[47]

> **CROWDS BUT NO SHEKINAH**
> For much that is undertaken by the Church He [the Holy Spirit] is not necessary. The Holy Ghost is no more needed to run bazaars, social clubs, institutions, and picnics, than He is to run a circus. When the Church is run on the same lines as a circus, there may be crowds, but there is no Shekinah. -- Samuel Chadwick, *The Way To Pentecost*

Vital truths such as Inerrancy, Substitution, Illumination, Regeneration, Sanctification and Separation that may in fact stir controversy or may require a change in lifestyle are being set aside in order for the Church to conform to the secular world's mindset that condones existentialism, the humanistic teaching that suggests there are no religious, ethical, or moral absolutes. This teaching provides the impetus for opening the door of compromise that approves of abortion of the unborn, gay marriage, infidelity in marriage, hedonism, and narcissism in society. If this teaching is promoted from the seminary level to the pastor and then on down to the man in the pew, then it's just a matter of time before the Church itself is dismantled from the very foundation.

Tal Brooke observes that the Emerging Church is making doctrinal concessions that "exalt private experience while shying away from Absolute Truth. The ageless gospel, once and for all delivered to the saints, now becomes an outworn embarrassment that must be tinkered with to suit the latest skeptical audience. The reigning delusion of the moment is appropriated with Christian window dressing." Chuck Smith of Calvary Chapel agrees: "The great confusion that exists in the divergent positions of the Emergent Church results from their challenging the final authority of the Scriptures. When you no longer have a final authority, then everyone's ideas become as valid as the next person's, and it cannot help but end in total confusion and contradictions."[48]

Descending down the slippery slope at this rate has serious implications in the pulpit. While at one time a troubled church-goer would visit with their pastor to discuss issues of unfaithfulness or immorality or a violation of ethical standards—or simply because they are despondent over life's cares—will instead go to today's family psychiatrist for counseling since the Church is rapidly conforming to the secular world. Rather than the Church being a vibrant spiritual fortress stocked with an arsenal of holiness and consecration to combat the attacks from its spiritual enemies so that the Christian can seek sanctuary therein, the Church has surrendered to the world's value system so that there's virtually no difference between the two. Therefore, people no longer have the confidence to go to her for help in time of crisis or spiritual need.

Undermining of Biblical Authority

Society must have a basis of authority in order to maintain law and order. In the court of law, we have two sources that are decisive factors in determining decisions that in turn effect the outcome of any legal argument. They are the Constitution and case law. These two critical components, together with the facts presented by the prosecution and defense, enable the judge and jury to render a fair and just decision. And so it is in spiritual matters. Society needs a basis of authority in order to render spiritual, ethical, and moral decisions. That authority is the Bible. When the Bible is undermined as the ultimate authority, then society will suffer the same fate we are experiencing in our courts of law where the Constitution is not only being challenged, but is being interpreted by liberal judges that render it impotent.

Six decades have passed since Samuel Chadwick penned the words that are an indictment on the Church. By extrapolating time we can see how his words have greater

---

CHRISTIANS HELD RESPONSIBLE

. . . the silent Christian leaders of America are more responsible for the moral decadence and breakdown of the republic than any other contributing force. Historically, do-nothing Christian leadership bears in part the responsibility for such atrocities as the Civil War and the holocaust of Jews in Germany. In either case, the majority of churches were not vociferous enough on the sinfulness of these actions to bring the evil to a swift conclusion. Those people who say, "I'm against abortion but I don't think you should have a law to stop it" are really saying the same thing as "I'm against slavery, but if you want to have a slave that's up to you."

If an action is morally wrong and degrading to the civil and human rights of any person, then it should be against the law. Laws are made to protect human and civil rights, and Christians should not be afraid to say so.

Jerry Falwell

value today: "The Church has lost the note of authority, the secret of wisdom and the gift of power, through persistent and willful neglect of the Holy Spirit of God. Confusion and impotence are inevitable when the wisdom and resources of the world are substituted for the presence and power of the Spirit of God."[49]

Chadwick's assessment of the Church of yesteryear is significantly correct for this argument today. The machinery of today's Christian Church has developed into a well-tuned engine that runs without the need of the Holy Spirit. The anemic state of the Christian church in America can be summed up in the words of the great Christian patriarch, A. W. Tozer, who said, "If God were to take the Holy Spirit out of this world, most of what the church is doing would go right on, and nobody would know the difference." This condition is called backsliding.

The Backslidden Church

Backsliding is defined as:

> [The] Condition that results from spiritual apathy or disregard for the things of God, whether on the part of an individual or a group bound by a prior covenantal pledge of commitment to uphold the doctrine and commandments of the Lord. Backsliding includes departure from a good confession of faith and from the ethical standards prescribed for God's people in the Scriptures. To varying degrees, depending on the extent of neglect of God and his

commandments, the spiritually wayward experience a season of estrangement and abandonment from God and his people.[50]

Apathy that leads to backsliding into sinful behavior is the outworking of a lapse in faith. This lapse in faith produces muddled theology and, in turn, an erosion of values and a distorted view of one's philosophy on life. Evidence of this lapse of faith can be seen in the warped views on doctrinal issues where fifty-two percent of all adults do not believe the Bible is totally accurate in all of its teachings. Regarding salvation, over sixty percent of the American population believes that if a person demonstrates good works they will go to heaven. Over sixty-two percent of the population who are unchurched consider themselves "Christian" despite the fact that they do not attend a church. More than sixty percent of the unchurched say that Satan is not a living being but simply a symbol of evil. More than fifty percent of those polled believe that Christ was s sinner. These statistics indicate that the corporate Church of today is experiencing a crisis of faith and in serious trouble when a rudimentary study in the Bible would easily substantiate any and all of these claims to the contrary.

The backslidden church will be held responsible to give an account to God for the present conditions in our nation. This backslidden behavior is both a divine chastisement and a rebuke for sin from God and will require repentance and a cleansing for the Church. Unless repentance and a cleansing occurs, the backsliding condition will continue to deteriorate leaving the Lord of Heaven no alternative but to mete out divine chastisement. This cycle is illustrated throughout the book of Jeremiah and Hosea with covenant Israel reminding us that God will not be mocked, nor will He allow apostasy to go unpunished in His bride, the Church. When the new trinity of Attendance, Buildings, and Cash replace the basic purpose of the Church—to proclaim the Word of God to reach the souls of men—the Church has reached the place where it has a neutral testimony. Neutrality, or "lukewarmness" is condemned in Scripture (Revelation 3:16) and tantamount to heresy. Dante penned these words in *The Inferno*, "The hottest places in Hell are reserved for those who, in times of moral crisis, maintain their neutrality." When the Church equivocates in their view toward absolute truth in matters such as homosexuality, divorce, pornography, abortion, the breakdown of the family—and simply sits on the sidelines allowing the freight train of compromise to run them over—then what the Church is really saying is, "we don't want to be disturbed." To this kind of Church, God has become impersonal. Historically, any nation that adopts an impersonal god is inevitably left to their own device which rapidly deteriorates into anarchy where everyone does what is right in their own eyes.

Gagging the Church

What the corporate Church of America can expect when it turns away from the God of the Bible and replaces Him with an impersonal god—one who has no influence on the lives of its citizens—is to be left defenseless before the secular world. In turn, the secular world with its liberal judges and liberal, left-wing celebrities routinely silence or gag the Church so that persons such as the outspoken thug, Rosie O'Donnell, can state, "Radical Christianity is just as threatening as radical Islam in a country like America where we have separation of church and state."[51] Several weeks later, the self-proclaimed homosexual recording artist, Elton John, stated that organized religion must be banned.

Hollywood moguls who produced the TV show, "The Book of Daniel," depict an Episcopal priest named Daniel as a drug addict with a drug dealing daughter and a homosexual son. The show is devoid of any guilt or conscience and religion seems to make no difference in the lives of the members and leaders of this congregation.

In Rome, we find the pop star Madonna who reached stardom by singing, "Like a Virgin" performing on stage during her "Confessions Tour," where she hung on a mirrored cross and wore a crown of thorns.

These acts are nothing short of blasphemy!

When these stunts and statements are made toward the Christian faith, they not only offend God, but are a threatening insult to the Church.

Can you imagine what would have happened if these statements or acts were done to offend Islam? Rosie and Madonna's homes would have been bombed and Elton John's partner would have been summarily executed in front of him.

But to offend the Church, that's OK and cool. Why?

Because nobody expects the Church to do anything about it.

Why wasn't there a public outrage (in a non-violent protest) like the reaction from the Mohammed carton when

Dr. Ralph D. Curtin

Hollywood brought us the heretical *DaVinci Code?*
Because the Church is gagged by its own compromise.

Heretical Churches

When so-called Christian churches promote the very thing that the Bible condemns in both the Old and New Testaments, then the Church deserves to lose its protection from God as heretical churches. Such is the case with the Presbyterian Church (U.S.A.):

> The Washington office of the Presbyterian Church (U.S.A.) is exhorting its members to press for changes in state and federal laws to recognize "same gender unions" and to require "all civil unions licensed and solemnized under state law to apply in all federal laws that provide benefits, privileges, and/or responsibilities to married person."[52]

The Episcopal Church (ECUSA) consecrated and ordained an openly homosexual bishop (V. Gene Robinson) and allows him to preach "his" gospel at a church in New Hampshire without any incrimination. Pro-homosexual churches such as the United Church of Christ and the Christian Church (Disciples of Christ) are rejecting traditional Christianity and caving in to society's demands to neutralize the central message of the Scriptures—to live a life that honors God—a brazen step toward depravity that will bring divine judgment.

South African Anglican Archbishop Desmond Tutu, who called for the church to fully accept homosexuality said, "We should celebrate sex as a wonderful gift of God. We should accept different sexual orientations. God made us who we are."[53] These homosexual offerings are not coming from the liberal "left" but from so-called Christian leaders in high positions of authority! Again, if this is what is being preached from the pulpit, what can we expect from the man in the pew?

With this kind of "church" mentality and "philosophy of ministry," is it any wonder that the Church stood by and did nothing when Roe V. Wade was an issue before the Supreme Court in 1973? Even though the majority of Americans were against abortion, "the Supreme Court arbitrarily ruled that abortion was legal, and overnight they overthrew the state laws and forced onto American thinking not only that abortion was legal, but that it was ethical."[54] Where were the Christians in the corporate church at that time? The Christian theologians and lawyers? Where were they? Why weren't they standing on the wall blowing the trumpets loud and clear warning of society's shift toward pluralism, relativism, and humanism?

In his seminal work, *Whatever Happened To The Human Race?*, Francis A. Schaeffer proclaimed in his

> **DOING NOTHING?**
> If we stand by and do nothing then millions of children will not be born.
> Nancy McDonald, Exec. Director of Hope Pregnancy Ctr., Davie, FL

argument against humanism that included abortion and

euthanasia, that for humanity to do nothing is to in fact endorse the act. "If we sit back and do nothing, our mere passivity and apathy will lead to actively evil results by removing resistance to those who are active and nonapathetic."[55] Likewise, for the Church to sit back and do nothing is complicity.

A parallel can be drawn from the Nazi Holocaust experience. In order for the Nazi war machine to accomplish their goals, they needed the cooperation of every sector of German society. "The bureaucrats drew the definitions and decrees, the churches gave evidence of Aryan descent, the postal authorities carried the messages of definition, expropriation, denaturalization and deportation. A place of execution was made available to the Gestapo and the SS by the Wehrmacht. To repeat, the operation required and received the participation of every major social and political and *religious* institution of the German Reich"[56] (emphasis added). If we have learned anything from this experience, it is that we have learned nothing from this experience. This adage when applied to the Church is a somber epitaph that reads: The Church doesn't want to be disturbed. By doing nothing, we are agreeing with society's dismantling of the very bulwark of our nation's Christian heritage and giving intellectual assent to the ultimate criminalization of Christianity.

The Criminalization of Christianity

Janet Folger is correct in her assessment of the precarious predicament of the Church when it dares to accuse the homosexual movement of its offense to God. Her research revealed that other nations, (while believing that America will soon follow their path), such as Sweden have outlawed quoting from the Bible if it offends homosexuals. She wrote: "Pastors will go to jail for speaking about homosexuality from their own pulpits in their own churches."[57] Folger cites a Pentecostal pastor in Sweden who was sentenced to a month in prison under a law against incitement after he was found guilty of offending homosexuals in a sermon. The prosecutor appealed the decision, demanding that the pastor be given a more severe sentence claiming, "When he started reading Bible verses about homosexuality, he crossed the line."[58]

Folger adds in her indictment against liberality that priests and bishops in Dublin are being warned that if they distribute the Vatican's statement on homosexual marriages, they can be imprisoned. Incidents such as these have given impetus to the movement here in the United States for clergymen to seek liability insurance to protect themselves from being prosecuted under pending Hate-Speech laws. Unfortunately, the Church has only voiced a minor protest to the pending legislation that will place even greater restrictions on preaching God's Word. And as Folger said, ". . . in any campaign, if an attack goes unanswered, it is assumed to be true." If the Church does not speak out against the onslaught against biblical values, the liberal media and the secular world assumes the Church agrees with their standards and accordingly pushes the margins further.

If the Church does not speak out against these atrocities now, we will be silenced later in courts of law.

Dr. Ralph D. Curtin

Silencing the Christians

Radical Left-Wing movements such as the Human Rights Campaign have taken up the crusade to rid the English language of the word "abomination" because the biblical word is used to describe homosexual practices in the sight of the Lord. Folger has spoken truth, "Christians are the only group still in the closet," when attesting to the impotence of the Church that has remained uninvolved in the political process. So, then we have no defense when laws are changed silencing the Christian. Further proof of the silencing of Christians is found where verbal prayer has been rendered unconstitutional in schools and no reading of the Bible during free time in schools. In addition, no Bible or books that deal with Christianity are allowed in the classroom library. In public forums, the name of "Jesus" is forbidden to be spoken.

Prior to 1962 when prayer was taken out of school, the problems teachers had were: talking, chewing gum, making noise, and running in the halls. After 1962 when prayer was removed, the problems were rape, robbery, assault, burglary, arson, bombing, and murder.[59] Yes, bumper stickers abound with lines like: "As long as there are tests in school, there will be prayer." And, "When prayer was removed from schools, guns were brought in." But bumper stickers aren't enough to change public opinion satisfactorily to bring about the necessary change in laws that are presently silencing Christians. The corporate Church must speak up, protest, and get involved to bring about change. Colson makes this point when quoting Martin Niemoller:

In Germany they came first for the Communists, and I didn't speak up because I wasn't a Communist. Then they came for the Jews, and I didn't speak up because I wasn't a Jew. Then they came for the trade unionists, and I didn't speak up because I wasn't a trade unionist. Then they came for the Catholics, and I didn't speak up because I was a Protestant. Then they came for me, and by that time no one was left to speak up[60].

It is apparent that the Christian Church— in the constant barrage over biblical values—a maelstrom of change in ethics—and a hostile societal environment—is losing the war. So what will it take for the Church to speak up and marshal their forces of Christian soldiers in a non-violent way to take back American's Christian heritage? A cataclysm in the Church? Divine intervention? Erwin Lutzer of Moody Church has these words to say regarding the Church: "...there are times when God no longer takes up the cause of His people. When we refuse to repent of our own sins, God might refuse to come to our aid and let us be defeated. This is why we must turn to Him as families, as churches, and as individuals. Without repentance for our own sins, we cannot expect to win our cultural wars. I believe very deeply that only God can save us now."[61]

But will God save the sleeping Church?

Yes, I too believe He can and will, *if the Church repents of its sin*. If not, I believe the same fate promised to Israel will come upon the Church:

But if you turn away and forsake the decrees and commands I have given you and go off to serve other gods and worship them, then I will uproot Israel from my land, which I have given them, and will reject this temple I have consecrated for my Name. I will make it a byword and an object of ridicule among all peoples. And though this temple is now so imposing, all who pass by will be appalled and say, "Why has the Lord done such a thing to this land and to this temple?" People will answer, "Because they have forsaken the LORD the God of their fathers, who brought them out of Egypt, and have embraced other gods, worshiping and serving them—that is why he brought all this disaster on them" (2 Chronicles 7:19-22).

But it's not too late.

CHAPTER 4
Sleeping Together

Woe to the obstinate children, declares the LORD, to those who carry out plans that are not mine, forming an alliance, but not by my Spirit, heaping sin upon sin; who go down to Egypt without consulting me; who look for help to Pharaoh's protection to Egypt's shade for refuge. But Pharaoh's protection will be to your shame . . .

The Prophet Isaiah 30:1-3

Biblical history has demonstrated that when Israel sought alliances with outside nations, their quest invariably led to compromised values followed by idolatry and subsequent punishment from Jehovah. When the nation of Babylon, under King Nebuchadnezzar, threatened Israel, Jehovah advised Jeremiah to warn the Israelites that they should not seek refuge in Egypt (Jeremiah 42:15-16). When they dismissed the warning as trivial so they could continue their wicked idolatrous practices, Jehovah sent King Nebuchadnezzar with a vengeance to Egypt to destroy them in the very place they sought sanctuary (Jeremiah 44:26-27; 46:26).

The High Places

High places were altars of worship of the Canaanite religion, and the conquering Israelites were commanded to destroy them when they entered Canaan (Nu. 33:52; Deut. 12:2; 33:29). The Canaanites were known for their fertility cults as well as their licentious and immoral behavior (Hosea 4:11-14; Jer. 3:2). Archeologists have unearthed evidence of sacred pillars and poles that many believe represented phallic symbols and chambers for cultic prostitution in honor of the heathen deities they worshiped. At Gezer, firstborn babies were slain and their bodies placed in jars near the high place (Isaiah 57:5).

Although the Mosaic prescription was intended to safeguard Israel from this idolatrous alliance and corruption, history has shown that Israel emulated the Canaanites through the introduction of the Canaanite high places into their worship practices. Jehovah commanded the Israelites to worship at one altar, the altar He chose, that is, the Wilderness Tabernacle or Solomon's Temple, while the worship of Jehovah at satellite locations that mimicked the Canaanites was condemned. The codicil being that during times of inaccessibility (after the fall of Shiloh or prior to the completion of Solomon's Temple, I Kings 3:2-4; 2 Chron. 1:3) the worship on satellite altars was permitted.

Unfortunately, Israel was determined to stay in bed with the pagan gods of the heathen world. Solomon took this practice to extremes by erecting high places for his heathen wives (I Kings 11:1-8), whereas Hezekiah broke them down (2 Kings 18:4, 22); then Manasseh in his idolatrous orgy re-erected them (2 Kings 21:3). They were again destroyed by Josiah (2 Kings 23:5, 8, 13). The prophets denounced the high places (Ezekiel 6:3) so that the emphasis for worship would be at God's designated place, Mount Zion (Isa. 2:2-3; 8:18; Joel 2:1; 3:17; Amos 1:2; Micah 4:1-2).

Throughout the Book of Judges, the cycle of Israel's unfaithfulness by forming alliances with heathen nations is evident. High places to the god Baal were not only tolerated, but became part of Israel's worship system (Judges 2:10-19). This in turn brought retribution from God. The cycle:

1. *Rebellion:* After the death of Joshua and a new generation was born, they no longer had any allegiance to the God of Israel, so they rebelled against Him by doing evil in His eyes by serving the "Baals" of the heathen nations around them (cf. Judges 3:7).

2. *Retribution:* Jehovah punished Israel by handing them over to overpowering raiders who plundered them (Judges 6:1, 25-26).

3. *Repentance:* When God raised up a judge, the people returned to the Lord who gave them victory over their enemies. But when the judge died, the people returned to their evil ways.

4. *Restoration:* While the judge lived, Israel enjoyed a period of peace and prosperity, but it was short-lived since

the heart of people was to refuse to give up their

evil practices and stubborn ways (Judges 2:19).

Whenever Israel consorted with pagan gods it led them to compromise their standard of spirituality. When they substituted heathen gods in alternative places of worship, Jehovah proclaimed through Jeremiah: "You have as many gods as you have towns, O Judah; and the altars you have set up to burn incense to that shameful god Baal are as many as the streets of Jerusalem" (Jeremiah 11:13).

Herein is a striking parallel to the Church.

Egypt metaphorically represents the world (cf. Acts 7:39) to which covenant Israel was warned not to seek shelter or to form an association. The Church can be equated to covenant Israel (although it did not theologically replace it) who has joined in partnership with the forces of this world (and often sought protection from it rather than God), placing the Church at risk for judgment. If the Church insists on seeking alliances and protection from the world to which God views as an act of fornication, theoretically then, God can issue a divorce decree, freeing Him from the obligation to protect His Church.

It will be shown that not only does the Church tolerate the "high places" but is determined to form alliances with the world.

The High Places In The Church

Organized religion has always played an important part in civilization's history. In the ancient world it was a powerful force. Pagan cultures worshipped male and female deities, high and low gods, assemblies of gods, priests and priestesses, temples, and embraced the sacrificial system of appeasing their gods. The forces of nature that the ancient world thought they could understand or control were considered supernatural powers to be worshipped.

Polytheism dominated the ancient world where more than one god was worshipped, usually in the form of representative idols such as statues or images to characterize the powers they worshipped. Today, the Church is worshipping more than one god.

Observing the worship practices of several gods is instrumental to our discussion.

Baal

The Canaanite god most often referred to is Baal, which means "lord" or "master." The word can be used as a title for any person who owned something or any god considered to be a lord or master. As a god who symbolized the productive forces of nature, Baal was worshipped with much sensuality (Num. 22:41; Judges 2:13; I Kings 16:31-32).[62]

> **GOD NO; DALAI LAMA, YES**
> In the Florida Sun Sentinel of September 19, 2004, the photo of the Dalai Lama appeared at the Nova Southeastern University before 10,000 Floridians to hear his philosophy on life. The report added that officials at the college allowed the unveiling of a "prominent symbol...the 600 pound brass prayer wheel on the stage."
> Why wasn't there an objection voiced by the Church when Judge Roy Moore was forced to remove the image of the Ten Commandments from his courtroom while a pagan religious symbol can be treated with reverence right here in our America?

This god of sensuality has infiltrated the Church where, as Stedman writes, "Baal worship is manifested in the rise of homosexuality as an acceptable lifestyle. It is behind the pornography that pervades almost every aspect of modern life."[63] Homosexuality and pornography have exerted tremendous force on the Church today, with its influence being felt in every aspect of American life. Many churches have caved into this mind set. Hollywood's dress and style is being emulated by the Christian who is seeking identification with the world. They have become modern altars with different idols. Coveting our time for our own purposes has become another graven image for the Christian of today whereas allotting time for the service of the church or for the Lord's people is simply not a priority.

Anat

Anat (Anath; a-nat) was the patroness of sex and war, the

paramour of Aliyan Baal. She is to be identified with the "queen of heaven" to whom Jews offered incense in Jeremiah's day (Jeremiah 44:19). Pornographic images have been unearthed from Palestinian sites at levels dating back from the second and first millennia B.C. Because of the degrading religion of the Canaanites, Moses and Joshua issued stern warnings to Israel. They realized the utterly debilitating effect of Canaanite cults upon the chaste morality and high spirituality demanded by the worship of Jehovah.[64]

The patroness of sex and pornographic images has taken up residence in many churches today. Online pornographic sites are often visited by clergy at hotels conducting church conventions and rampant in the private homes of many pastors. When society's moral censors raised the level of acceptance of "soft" porn on broadcast TV, the world found the Church sleeping. Hardly a peep was voiced by church leadership. Pornography and sexual themes continue to dominate cable TV networks and radio talk shows, feeding the appetite for unbridled lust and sexual purveyors—with increasing numbers being viewed by Church-goers.

Molech

Molech, a Semitic deity and god of the Ammonites, was particularly odious to Jehovah since he required human sacrifice (Lev. 18:21; 20:1-5). Palestinian excavations have uncovered evidences of infant skeletons in burial places around heathen shrines. Despite God's warning, Solomon built an altar to Molech at Topheth in the valley of Hinnom.[65] Tourists to modern-day Caesarea Philippi are escorted to the stone altars where children were sacrificed to pagan idols.

> **CONSERVATION REMINDER**
> Trafficking in threatened wildlife such as the tiger (Panthera tigris) is illegal. Though their medicinal value remains unproven, tiger bones are sold as pain relievers, tails for skin treatment, and genitals to boost virility. Poachers can earn more than the average annual salary from the kill of single tiger. Conservationists want this practice stopped — and well it should be. But what about conserving the unborn human? Where is the conservation foundation for them? Why isn't the killing of humans illegal?

With 280 abortions being performed each day in South Florida's murder mills alone, two million since Roe V. Wade and one million per year nationwide, the question about Church involvement must arise. If the Church mounted overwhelming, non-violent protests, and insisted on political change, there would be capitulation by civil leadership. But with the "I need to get my life back" mindset of the corporate Church—self being primary with education, career, family, or convenience being second—there is only a whimper of objection coming from the Church.

Numerous states in America (Florida being one of them) are competing for stem cell research facilities and programs that will bolster the state's employment as well as its tax revenue base by bringing in government and commercial funding.[66] *Stem cell research's testing matter is heavily dependent on human abortions.* This concept of bringing millions of dollars into a city's coffers from the outworking of a sinful enterprise is addressed in Acts 19 where the silversmith named Demetrius who made idols of Artemis (ar'te-mis), a god known among the Greeks as Artemis and among the Romans as Diana, saw his business going down the tubes when Paul preached Christ to the Ephesians. Demetrius argued that not only was his trade in jeopardy, but that the goddess Artemis would be disgraced. See the parallel? At times Artemis was a benevolent deity, a helping guide with luminous light by day and night. Her proper domain was that of nature, being a mighty huntress, sometimes chasing wild animals, sometimes dancing, playing, or bathing with her companions. Artemis (Diana) was also a protectress of youth, especially of her own sex.

While the Church remains impotent regarding the issue of abortion, abortion advocates will continue to forge ahead in their sales campaign heralding abortion as some kind of benevolent deity under the guise of medical research, public welfare, and humanitarian dollar assistance to social programs. However, as long as the Church adopts a spirit of tolerance toward this national sin that is tantamount to idolatry, God cannot bless this nation despite the many prayers for revival. God's word is very clear on this matter: "The sorrows of those who have bartered for another god will be multiplied" (Psalm 16:4).

The Church is allowing the unbelievers of this nation to dictate what teaching from God is appropriate to address the Church and America. The Church is afraid of offending anyone who is in sin when in reality we need to scare them into repentance.

Castor and Pollux

Castor (kas'tor) and Pol'lux (Gk. "sons of Jupiter") were twin gods representing sports figures worshipped at Sparta and Olympia with Hercules and other heroes (cf. Acts 28:11 KJV). Castor was a horse tamer and Pullux master of the art of boxing. They were ideal types of bravery and dexterity in fighting.[67]

To many sports enthusiasts in America, athletic heroes and their associate games have replaced their concept of God. The players are worshipped as champions and gladiators, men to be adored and copied. They have been placed on the high place as a god to be worshipped. To be emulated and sought after, where their names, their endorsements, and their old jerseys and worn-out cleats are considered by their fans as holy relics fetching huge dollar amounts on E-bay or other merchandising networks. A huge amount of Americans would rather attend a three-hour football game that cost them hundreds of dollars to see as well as hours to travel rather than spend one hour with God on a Sunday morning. Jim Cymbala comments on this American tragedy: "No attendance numbers can hide the fact that our new kind of Christianity is foreign to the Bible and grievous to the Holy Spirit. All over America, churchgoers chafe at Sunday morning service that runs an hour and ten minutes, but have no problem with three-hour football games on television."[68]

The Church has supported this mindset by offering special events on Super Bowl Sunday, martial arts programs and motorcycle clubs designed to draw the sport enthusiast into the church on the premise that they would not ordinarily come to church. Is this not a form of gimmickry? Where is the operation of the Holy Spirit to draw men unto God? To the Church? Where are the disciples who know the Word of God and share the Word with those who would come out to a sports event? Do we have to resort to "sales gimmicks" such as the commercial and secular world operates?

Where are the seven thousand who have not bowed the knee to Baal?

Let them stand up and be counted!

In antiquity, the pagan religion of Rome was a rite rather than a doctrine. In effect, the emperor declared: "this you must do, but you can think as you please." Roman worshippers believed they needed only to perform the proper ceremonies of religion, whether they understood them or not. As far as they were concerned, a hypocritical skeptic could be just as "religious" as a true believer, so long as he offered sacrifice in the temple of the gods.

Unless the corporate Church corrects its thinking, the average church-goer will simply follow the same path. They will come to church on Sunday, but think as they please, performing the proper ceremonies of religion, but lacking conviction and purpose. What is needed is the attitude of the first century Christian where both belief and behavior were vital, going hand in hand. Taking Jesus' words seriously that, "true worshipers shall worship the Father in spirit and truth" (John 4:23). In other words, what a Christian believed in his heart and mind, he would act out in his life.

Dr. Ralph D. Curtin

Historical Precedence

By looking back in history we can arrive at a reasonable measure of man's response to lessons learned. It has been said, "If there's anything we've learned from experience, it's that we've learned nothing from experience." The following tables should give the reader a measure of the direction America is headed and what we can expect:

The Destruction Of The Roman Empire[69]

    1. The undermining of the dignity and sanctity of the home

    2. Increasing taxes and spending of public money for bread and circuses (welfare and amusements)

    3. The mad craze for pleasure, with sports becoming more exciting and brutal

    4. The building of gigantic armaments, when the real enemy is the decadence of the people

    5. The decay of religion, with faith fading into mere form

America may not be experiencing all of the conditions listed in the fall of Rome, but many of them are apparent in our society, with the prospect of all of them being realized soon. But before the fall of Rome, there was an ancient civilization that the Bible describes to be more in line with what is happening in our present generation. The following table lists the reasons for their demise:

Similarities In Present World Condition With Antediluvian Society[70]

1. Preoccupation with physical appetites, Luke 17:27
2. Rapid advances in technology, Genesis 4:22
3. Grossly materialistic attitudes and interests, Luke 17:28
4. Uniformitarian philosophies, Hebrews 11:7
5. No concern for God in either belief or conduct, II Peter 2:5; Jude 15
6. Disregard for the sacredness of the marriage relationship, Matthew 24:38
7. Rejection of the inspired Word of God, I Peter 3:19
8. Population explosion, Genesis 6:1, 11
9. Widespread violence, Genesis 6:11, 13
10. Corruption throughout society, Genesis 6:12
11. Preoccupation with illicit sexual activity, Genesis 4:19; 6:2
12. Widespread words and thoughts of blasphemy, Jude 15
13. Organized Satanic activity, Genesis 6:1-4
14. Promulgation of systems and movements of abnormal depravity, Genesis 6:5, 12

The above tables describe the world's environment before God intervened to teach man a lesson. The demise of the

Dr. Ralph D. Curtin

Roman Empire and the destruction of all mankind (save eight persons) by a global flood is the outworking of society flouting their sinful behavior before a holy and loving God.

Sodom and Gomorrah

Our last illustration is found in Genesis 18-19 where Jehovah appeared to Abraham (Genesis 18:22) and warned that He was about to bring judgment on the cities of Sodom and Gomorrah for their wicked behavior, namely homosexuality (Genesis 19:5). Abraham entreats God for mercy and a bargaining session begins, ending when God agrees to spare the city for the sake of ten righteous: "The LORD said, If I find fifty righteous people in the city of Sodom, I will spare the whole place for their sake ... for the sake of ten, I will not destroy it" (Genesis 19:26, 32c).

It is clear in this passage that judgment was not about to come upon the cities because of the amount of wicked persons, but because of the lack of righteous persons.

This is the remedy to ward off judgment: that the righteous, the believers in the Lord who are sleeping with the unbelievers, will repent. The unbelievers are not the salt or the light and are not expected to act in a righteous manner.

The modern corporate Church is guilty of complicity in the downfall of our society because the Church has been called to be the "salt of the earth" and "the light of the world" (Matthew 5:13-14). Salt: to be the vital ingredient to preserve society from decay and rot; and light: to keep society from descending into the pit of darkness where the depravity of man is allowed to run its course. Without the preserving power of the Church, society's propensity toward debauchery will go unchecked.

Thus the notion that America will somehow implement a self-healing mechanism to bring society back on course seems as distant as the Andromeda galaxy. To think that the pendulum will naturally swing back and bring corrective measures into our moral fiber with the pervasive power of the high-tech popular culture, the mass media, the entertainment industry's role models, and godless academia is a mere pipe dream. William P. Barr observes:

> In the past, when societies deviate too far from sound moral principles, they end up paying such a high price that they ultimately recoil and are forced to re-evaluate the path they are on. So venereal diseases and AIDS is the price we pay, among many others, for sexual license. Violent crime and poverty is a price we pay for the breakdown of the family. So, in the past, societies have been driven back to their senses by the sheer cost of misconduct. But today, something is new. The state—which no longer sees itself as a moral institution, but as a secular one—takes on the role as the alleviator of bad consequences. The state is called upon to remove the inconvenience and costs of misconduct. So the reaction to diseases and illegitimacy is not sexual responsibility but handing out condoms. And the reaction to drug addiction is clean needles.
>
> While we think we are solving problems we are actually subsidizing them. And by lowering the cost

of misconduct, the government perpetuates it. The corrosive impact on society continues. And like most solutions that deal with symptoms rather than causes, it only makes matters worse.

Society is expecting the government to legislate morality when that responsibility has been given by God to the Church. Society's current problems are a reflection of the Church's weakness that is the out-working of its spiritual adultery—sleeping with the world.

The only thing necessary for evil to triumph is for good men to do nothing.
Edmund Burke, statesman, Orator, Political Thinker

LEGISLATING MORALITY
Morality is legislated every day from the vantage point of one value system or another. The question is not whether we will legislate morality, but whose morality we will legislate. Charles Colson, *Kingdoms in Conflict*, p. 279.

CHAPTER 5
Sleeping Pills

The bridegroom was a long time in coming, and they all became drowsy and fell asleep.

Jesus Christ, Matthew 25:5

> **IDOLATRY**
> It has been reported that after a Chinese man visited America that upon his return to China he was asked whether Americans worshipped idols. "Yes, they do," he reported. "They have three of them. In the winter they worship a fat man in a red suit. In the spring they worship a rabbit. And in the fall they sacrifice a turkey."

The Dutch Philosopher Baruch Spinoza once said, "Man builds his kingdoms in accord with his concept of God."[71] America has indeed built its kingdom based on its concept of God—the god of "isms." America is no longer a nation whose God is the God of the Bible, but an idolatrous nation with many false gods: humanism, atheism, materialism, hedonism, narcissism, existentialism, pluralism, relativism, secularism, and syncretism. These gods have tranquilized Americans and lulled them to sleep with a false peace. The

Church has not stimulated or challenged the unbelieving world because the Church itself is sleeping after ingesting a good dose of these secular sleeping pills.
And they have become very habit forming.

The Humanism Pill

Central to this argument is the fundamentals of the Humanist movement that was declared by the Supreme Court to be a religion. This was determined in 1961 in the case of Torcaso v. Watkins that specifically defines secular humanism as a religion equivalent to theistic and other nontheistic religions.[72] The following is the basic tenets of belief for the humanist:

The Humanist Manifesto

    a. Religious humanists regard the universe as self-existing and not created (*The foundation of humanism is evolution*).

    b. Humanism believes that man is a part of nature and that he has emerged as the result of a continuous process.

    c. Holding an organic view of life, humanists find that the traditional dualism of mind and body must be rejected.

    d. Humanism recognizes that man's religious culture and civilization, as clearly depicted by anthropology and history, are the product of a gradual development due to his interaction with his natural environment and with his social heritage. The individual born into a particular culture is largely molded to that culture.

e. Humanism asserts that the nature of the universe depicted by modern science makes unacceptable any supernatural or cosmic guarantees of human values (*Humanists reject God, the Bible and biblical morality.*).

f. Humanists are convinced that the time has passed for theism, deism, modernism, and several varieties of "new thought."

g. Religion consists of those actions, purposes, and experiences which are humanly significant. Nothing human is alien to the religious *(Including any form of sexual perversion.)*.

h. Religious humanism considers the complete realization of human personality to be the end of man's life and seeks its development and fulfillment in the here and now.

i. In place of the old attitudes involved in worship and prayer, the humanist finds his religious emotions expressed in a heightened sense of personal life and in a cooperative effort to promote social well-being.

j. A humanist will not acknowledge any uniquely religious emotions and attitudes of the kind hitherto associated with belief in the supernatural.

k. Humanists claim that man will learn to face the crisis of life (*an attempt to minimize death*) in terms of his knowledge of their naturalness and probability. Reasonable and manly attitudes will be fostered by education and supported by custom.

l. Believing that religion must work increasingly for joy in living, religious humanists aim to foster the creative in man and to encourage achievements that add to the satisfactions of life.

m. Religious humanism maintains that all associations and institutions exist for the fulfillment of human life. The intelligent evaluation, transformation, control, and direction of such associations and institutions with a view to the enhancement of human life are the purposes and programs of humanism. Certainly, religious . . . and communal activities must be reconstituted as rapidly as experience allows in order to function effectively in the modern world (*An open attack on the Church and Christians.*).

n. The humanists are firmly convinced that existing acquisitive and profit-motivated society has shown itself to be inadequate (*Opposed to American free enterprise system*) and that a radical change in methods, controls, and motives must be instituted. A socialized and cooperative economic order must be established to the end that the equitable distribution of the means of life be possible. The goal of humanism is a free and universal (One-world government) society in which people voluntarily and intelligently cooperate for the common good. Humanists demand a shared life in a shared world (Socialistic communism).

o. Humanists assert that this movement will (a)

affirm life rather than deny it; (b) seek to elicit the possibilities of life, not flee from it; and (c) endeavor to establish the conditions of a satisfactory life for all, not merely for the few (emphasis added) .[73]

Summarizing the fifteen principles of humanism we can say that the humanist religion has its own set of doctrinal teachings:

1. Disbelief in God
2. Belief in evolution
3. Rejection of absolute morals
4. Deification of man as supreme
5. Belief in the innate goodness of men to govern the world equitably.

Schaeffer defined humanism as,

> ... Man beginning from himself, with no knowledge except what he himself can discover and no standards outside of himself. In this way Man is the measure of all things, as the Enlightenment expressed it. . . they have reduced Man to even less than his natural finiteness by seeing him only as a complex arrangement of molecules, made complex by blind chance. Instead of seeing him as something great that is significant even in his sinning, they see Man in his essence only as an intrinsically competitive animal that has no other basic operating principle than natural selection brought about by the

strongest, the fittest, ending on top. And they see Man as acting in this way both individually and collectively as society. [74]

This humanism sleeping pill has many side effects. Man has done away with sociological standards with no fixed base laws in which a society can live with one another. There is no standard for what is sociologically good for society at any given moment. This unfortunately leads man to arbitrarily decide what becomes law. This logic is played out in the following statement by humanists in their neo-religious tenets against Christianity and the God of the Bible:

> First, God has no role in the physical world, and second, except for the laws of probability and cause and effect, there is no organizing principle in the world, and no purpose. Thus, there are no moral or ethical laws that belong to the nature of things, no absolute guiding principles for human society...The mechanistic view of life has perhaps only one tangible implication for ethics—we should feel freer to adapt our morality to new social situations . . . ethical choices are likely to become more difficult, not because people are less moral but because they will be unable to justify their choices with fairy tales.[75]

Thus, the Judeo-Christian view is now relegated to the category of "fairy tales."

The outworking of the humanism sleeping pill that has anesthetized society can be seen in the colleges of America today where the "reprogramming" of church and family values occurs during freshman indoctrination and orientation. During these sessions students' brains are washed with matters of humanistic and moral relativism teachings, along with tolerance, gay/lesbian/transgendered rights, postmodernism, and New age spirituality. The thinking that emerges from these think tanks (more like cesspools) is: "'It's OK to have premarital sex, just use a condom. Homosexuality is normal, just accept it,' *and* lectures and writings such as 'America deserved the terrorist attacks of 9/11.'"

> **JOHN EDWARDS ON ABORTION**
> Democratic 2008 presidential hopeful, John Edwards, announced that he had selected Kate Michelman, who served for almost 20 years as president of the National Abortion Rights Action League, as a senior campaign advisor conducting outreach to women voters. Edwards seems determined to stick to his pro-abortion guns. National Right to Life Committee political director, Karen Cross, said Edwards' choice of Michelman "underscores not only his strong pro-abortion stance, but also his strong ties to the pro-abortion movement."
> --Priya Abraham, *World* Magazine; January 20, 2007; p. 30.

According to Tim LaHaye, pastor and multi-million book author of the *Left-Behind* series, no humanist should be permitted to hold public office. He writes: "No humanist is qualified to hold any government office in America–United

States senator, congressman, cabinet member, State Department employee, or any other position that requires him to think in the best interest of America. He is a socialist one-worlder first, an American second."[76]

Because the humanism movement views Bible-believing churches and moral-minded citizens as avowed enemies, the movement has deliberately used every method of espionage available to infiltrate the corporate Church to eliminate or minimize the threat. The weapon being used by the humanist has led to moral turpitude or failure. The corporate Church has bought into the humanist philosophy where humans are viewed as nothing more than animals with instincts of the cave men that have been restrained by biblical ethics and should be allowed to vent their full capacity for sexual enjoyment in the here and now. Evidence of this truth is seen where more than fifty-five percent of all Christian marriages are ending in divorce, mainly due to adultery and fornication. The corporate Church has also forsaken its code in the area of pornography. While at one time a *Playboy* magazine would be taboo to any clergyman or Christian, the Church has compromised this standard by allowing pornography to surreptitiously come into their homes through their PCs and TVs (Online, cable TV, DVDs, etc.). This is in addition to "chat rooms" that have become nothing more than "cruising lanes" for sexual purveyors—many of which are leaders in the Church who are of the erroneous thinking that God does not see what they are doing in the privacy of their own homes. The bottom line is that current studies show that traditional moral values upheld by Christians are continuing to lose ground.

And this sleeping pill has become very habit-forming.

The Atheism Pill

The Russian philosopher Alexander Solzhenitsyn once commented on the atrocity of the Bolshevik revolution where sixty million perished and said, "I could not put it more accurately than to repeat, 'Men have forgotten God'— that's why all this happened." We can extrapolate on this statement and add the Nazi Holocaust and the Roe v. Wade Holocaust as the outworking of the religion of atheism—the forgetting of God. Atheism is the natural product of the religion of secular philosophy, namely, humanism.

Humanism has been shown to be indeed a religion, but few recognize atheism as a "religion." But indeed, it is as well. When Judge Myron Thompson declared that the display of the Ten Commandments is illegal, he asked and answered, "Can the state acknowledge God? No." By doing so, he has declared America to be an atheist nation. This act was in direct violation of the First Amendment that reads, "Congress shall make no law respecting an establishment of religion." So Judge Thompson in effect has instituted as the law of the land the religion of atheism, which says there is no God. From that day forward, our entire judicial system must be based on the religion of atheism.

Atheism is defined as the disbelief in the existence of any deities. This contrasts with theism, the belief in a God or gods. Variations on this theme include, "the deliberate rejection of theism," and "the simple absence of belief in deities." G. K. Chesterton said in regard to atheism, "The danger when men stop believing in God is not that they'll believe in nothing, but that they'll believe in anything." The act of believing in anything raises the issue of cause: that atheism is often related with immorality and evil, often being characterized as a willful and malicious repudiation of God or gods, where atheists are known to behave as though God, morals, ethics, and social responsibility did not exist; they abandoned duty and embraced hedonism. The French Catholic philosopher Etienne Borne supported this view by saying, "Practical atheism is not the denial of the existence of God, but complete godlessness of action; it is a moral evil, implying not the denial of the absolute validity of the moral law but simply rebellion against that law."[77] Durant enforces this key principle where he adds, "There is no significant example in history before our time, of a society successfully maintaining moral life without the aid of religion."[78]

One could argue then, that the existence and rise of evil is directly linked to atheism.

If America were a nation of state gods, that is a nation ruled by so-called deities such as in the time of the Roman

> **CARL SAGAN'S ATHEISTIC STATEMENT**
> Carl Sagan's arrogant statement on public television—made without any scientific proof for the statement—to 140 million views: "The cosmos is all that is or ever was or ever will be." He opened the series, *Cosmos*, with this essential creedal declaration and went on to build every subsequent conclusion on it. --- Francis A. Schaeffer, *The Christian Manifesto*, Wheaton, IL; Crossway Books; 1993; p. 44.

emperors, the atheists would be executed for sedition because they rejected the god of the nation. In the first century, many Christians were executed because of their rejection of the Roman gods, and "heresy" and "godlessness" were serious capital offenses following the rise of Christianity. This, too, was the fate of Socrates who was called an *atheos* (godless) and sentenced to death for impiety on the grounds that he questioned the state gods. Instrumental in the rise of Communism and Nazism were the German philosophers Karl Marx and Friedrich Nietzsche who denied the existence of deities and were critical of religion. Modern atheists include notables such as Katharine Hepburn and Woody Allen.

  Although atheists only make up about four percent of the world's population, their impact on society when viewed through the eyes of the humanist, have a profound effect on the population. In the mind of the atheist, holding a variety of ethical beliefs adversely affects ethics that leads to moral nihilism that teaches that morality is meaningless. Since morality is based on belief derived from God, without the belief in God, morality cannot be attained.

Citing modern scientific discoveries in the field of cosmology, astronomy, and biology, the atheist now holds that no deity could be involved in the universe. Their tenet states that science has since eliminated the need for appealing to supernatural explanations for the maintenance of planet earth and the cosmos.

Attacks on the Bible are common among atheists. Their theological claims often go from the specific and observable (including scientific findings) to the general and metaphysical:

Within the framework of scientific rationalism one arrives at the belief in the nonexistence of God, not because of certain knowledge, but because of a sliding scale of methods. At one extreme, we can confidently rebut the personal God of Creationists on firm empirical grounds: science is sufficient to conclude beyond reasonable doubt that there never was a worldwide flood and that the evolutionary sequence of the Cosmos does not follow either of two versions of Genesis. The more we move toward a deistic and fuzzily defined God, however, the more scientific rationalism reaches into its toolbox and shifts from empirical science to logical philosophy informed by science.[79]

Many atheists have argued against the Christian apologetic that uses both the cosmological and teleological arguments that support the existence of God and the Creation account. In addition to dismissing these solid arguments, they conveniently disregard the Laws of Thermodynamics that categorically support the Bible's account of Creation while discrediting the evolutionary claims.

Further repudiation of the atheists' claim:

1. Most theologians considered the existence of God so self-evident and universally-accepted that whether or not true atheism even existed was frequently questioned. This view is based on theistic innatism, the belief that all people believe in God from birth and that atheists are simply in denial. [80]

2. It is asserted that atheists are quick to believe in God in times of crisis—that atheists will readily make deathbed confessions or during a time of national crisis (i.e. September 11, 2001; Hurricane Katrina, etc.).[81]

3. Since the existence of deities cannot be proven or disproved with certainty, it requires a leap of faith to conclude that deities do or do not exist.

4. It is commonly held that the lack of belief in a deity who administers justice may lead to moral or ethical shifts in society and that atheism makes life meaningless and miserable.[82]

The outworking of the atheism sleeping pill can be seen in today's headlines where a noted film director, James Cameron (*Titanic, Aliens*), would produce a documentary denying the resurrection of Christ based on the spurious findings of ossuaries in a cave outside Jerusalem. If the Church were not impotent, then why wasn't there an outcry from every evangelical leader and church-goer demanding a retraction and apology? One would think that when the entire foundation of Christianity was being attacked that the Christian Church would react in such a way that these assailants would be silenced and humiliated.

Explain why these apostates don't pick on Hinduism, or

FILLING THE VOID

People turn to drugs and alcohol because they don't have a clue as to why they're alive. Others turn to career achievements, or pleasure, or materialism ... something, anything to fill the void. But it doesn't work. God created them to worship and enjoy him forever, but this awareness has been stolen from their consciousness. —Jim Cymbala, *Fresh Wind, Fresh Fire*.

Buddhism, or Mormonism, or the Jehovah Witnesses, or Darwinism, or the Baha'i Faith, or Eckankar, or Pokemon? If this were an attack on Islam and Mohammed, James Cameron and his company would be severely marginalized. But when it comes to the Christian Church and the Bible, anything goes. There is only a "slap on the hand." So the attack by atheists on the Church will continue unabated.

The Materialism Pill

Common among modern day Church-goers is the worship of material things, where their luxurious home, high-performance automobile, or expensive camera has become an idol that is frequently put before the worship of God. Possessions control the worshipper and have become their master. They polish their plasma-screen or wardrobe and display it like it was some deity. Should it be damaged, the worshipper is often inconsolable. This "god" or the tangible reality reflected in our lives is an idol worth rebuking.

The argument for Americans living in the here and now in the world of materialism was advanced by Sir Julian Huxley (1887-1975) who clarified the dilemma (of materialism) by acknowledging, though he was an atheist, that somehow or other—against all that one might expect—a person functions better if he acts as though God exists. "So," the argument goes, "God does not in fact exist, but act as if He does!" In other words, according to Huxley, you can function properly only if you live your whole life upon a lie. You act as if God exists, which to the materialist is false.[83]

The desire for material possessions has a magnetic grip on America and the corporate Church. The drive to outdo, out-achieve our parents has mutated over the generations so that the Busters (those born from 1965-1977) are infatuated with the desire to out-class their parents, the Boomers (those born from 1946-1964), with as many possessions as can be acquired—even if it means taking an equity loan on their home or working two jobs. This rational emerged from the fact that the Busters have grown accustomed to the good life, and believe it is their right to enjoy continued comfort. This attitude gave rise to the bumper sticker philosophy, "He who dies with the most toys, wins."

The spiritual, ethical, and moral condition of today's society can be directly attributed to the sleeping pills the corporate Church has ingested over the past four decades. The Church is drowsy, nodding off and almost asleep—buying into the world of materialism at an alarming rate. Just imagine for a moment if Christ's words that were spoken to the Rich Young Man were to become a requirement for discipleship today: "If you want to be perfect ('mature'), go, sell your possessions and give to the poor, and you will have treasure in heaven. Then come, follow me" (Matthew 19:21). It is my belief that a great majority of today's Christians would react the same way the Rich Young Man did: "When the young man heard this, he want away sad, because he had great wealth," (Matthew 19:22). Christians are entitled to much more than selling our souls as we pant after the material things rather than following after the Christ who leads us to the cross.

With the Church buying into the world's system of humanism, atheism, and materialism, along with other sleeping pills such as hedonism, narcissism, relativism, pluralism, secularism, syncretism and ecumenism, it is systematically losing its potency to retard the advancing spread of the very philosophies that have brought other civilizations to ruin. These compromises have in turn produced other "isms" that are plaguing the Church: fearism, phobiaism, and sedentaryism. For this, there can be no remedy unless the Church repents of its addiction to these sleeping pills. This explains Christ's admonition: "Nevertheless when the Son of man cometh, shall he find faith on the earth?" (Luke 18:8). The prognosis is clear: The longer Christ delays His return, the greater the falling away from His Church and the greater the decline of civilization.

The Hedonism Pill

Next in the line of "isms" is hedonism, the philosophy that teaches that man owes it to himself to derive as much pleasure out of experiences as possible, that all actions can be measured on the basis of pleasure and how little pain they produce. Most often, the hedonistic philosophy usually has a sexual or libidinal connotation; that is, allowing sexual instincts to have their full vent. A "libertine" is one who is morally or sexually unrestrained—free from the slavery of moral standards.

Early thinkers such as Sigmund Freud believed in psychological hedonism where his "life instinct" stated that people will pursue pleasure, but added that there were complexities and mechanisms in this theory that produced the "death instinct" that is, the desire for silence and peace, for calm and darkness, which causes men another form of happiness—namely producing a desire for death that can be attributed to the rise of suicides in America within the past decade, especially among American youth.

The infiltration of hedonism into the Church is readily visible: the craze to live a hedonistic life by both the adult and youth audience of today's churches is demonstrated by their infatuation with the media and the lives of celebrities. Christians have become besotted with the hero worship of TV and cinema personalities, emulating and copying them like never before in the history of the screen. Must the Church look to Brittany Spears and Russell Crowe for their heroes? Where are the Christian heroes? Where are Christian celebrities that we can model our lives after? Where are the Davids and Daniels of today that should be setting the example?

They are sleeping.

The Narcissism Pill

Narcissism, the art of self-love. The definition conveys excessive vanity, conceit, egotism, and simple selfishness— often displayed in an indifference to the plight of others. Narcissism breeds a society of constant competition were there are few allies with little transparency, nurturing the mentality, "every man for himself." This type of person unconsciously looks for a mirror image of themselves in others, seeking criteria of beauty or reproductive fitness in the context of self-reference. Studies have linked narcissism to related areas such as sexual expression and promiscuity. Narcissists constantly look to acquire status symbols, thrive on defensiveness, and reject a sense of community. They are consumed with crazes such as their appearance, clothes, weight-loss campaigns, wrinkle-free creams, aerobics, hair restorers—resolute in their quest to hold onto the hair and figure they had when they were in high school or college in an attempt to arrest advancing age.

The Christian is admonished to refrain from narcissism:

> 1. We do not dare to classify or compare ourselves with some who commend *themselves*. When they measure *themselves* by *themselves* and compare *themselves* with *themselves*, they are not wise (2 Corinthians 10:12, emphasis added).
>
> 2. Nobody should seek *his own* good, but the good of others (1 Corinthians 10:24, emphasis added).

But rather than be the "salt" Christ calls us to be and thereby set an example to the secular world, the Christian, in order to "identify" with the world around him or her, has compromised their standards by becoming just like it. Yet, it appears that this is what may be expected of people in the last days on earth:

> But mark this: There will be terrible times in the last days. People will be *lovers of themselves*, lovers of money, boastful, proud, abusive, disobedient to their parents, ungrateful, unholy, without love, unforgiving, slanderous, without self-control, brutal, not lovers of the good, treacherous, rash, conceited, lovers of pleasure rather than lovers of God—having a form of godliness but denying its power. Have

nothing to do with them (2 Timothy 3:1-5, emphasis added).

What we see happening in the Church is exactly what Paul predicted would happen in the secular world, that "People will be lovers of themselves. . ." And he goes on to describe the very symptoms the Church is experiencing, ". . . being lovers of self, to lovers of money . . . without self-control . . . lovers of pleasure rather than lovers of God." What the Church is called to do is found in Philippians 2:3-4: *"Do nothing out of selfish ambition or vain conceit, but in humility consider others better than yourselves. Each of you should look not only to your own interests, but also to the interests of others"* (emphasis added).

So why isn't the Church setting the proper example? Because the Church is sleeping.

The Existentialism Pill

Existentialism is a philosophical movement in which individual human beings are understood as having full responsibility for creating the meanings of their own lives. This movement is the direct descendent of atheism where the meaning of human life is ascribed to man defining his reality totally apart from any supernatural intervention. This philosophy promotes the denial of any moral absolute. Typical to the existentialist mindset that discards the supernatural hand of the sovereign God is Kierkegaard's portrayal of the Young Man in *Repetition*:

> How did I get into the world? Why was I not asked about it, why was I not informed of the rules and

regulations but just thrust into the ranks as if I had been bought by a peddling shanghaier of human beings? Why should I be involved? Isn't it a matter of choice . . . where is the manager—I have something to say about this. Is there no manager? To whom shall I make my complaint?

Kierkegaarrd, the nineteenth-century thinker, attempts to counter the feeling of deep anxiety of human existence where the person feels that there is no purpose to life, with nothing at its core. He therefore embraced "existence" as the sole purpose in life. As long as one exists, there is purpose. Existentialism asserts that people actually make decisions based on what has meaning to them rather than what is rational. This of course would negate any principle found in the Bible since it would not make any sense or meaning to the existentialist since the Bible has a spiritual, ethical, and moral base to it, which in the mind of the existentialist, would not have any meaning. Existentialism tends to view human beings as indifferent subjects in a ridiculous universe, in which meaning is not provided by any supernatural or natural order, but rather created by human beings' actions and interpretations. In the final analysis, existentialism holds that people conceal their true heart that believes in the meaninglessness of life and their use of diversion to escape from boredom.

While Viktor Frankl's psychological existentialism may bring a person to the conclusion that even in the worst imaginable circumstances, life can be assigned a worthwhile meaning, and that all human beings have a will to find that meaning, this philosophy has serious flaws when compared to the principles found in the Bible. Namely, all meaning and purpose apart from knowledge of God is a mere exercise in futility since man cannot be separated from his circumstances or environment without succumbing to a state meaninglessness. Man was created to have a relationship with his Creator-God, and without that relationship, life *is* meaningless.

Existentialism has leached out into the mainstream of Christianity and taken a toehold in the Church. This is evidenced by the lack of spiritual, ethical, and moral convictions among the Church-goers of today.

My personal research that spans two decades of teaching in seminaries to students of various denominations reveals that the modern pew-warmer knows very little about what they believe, and they are very wishy-washy when it comes to Bible doctrine. Barna research has labored extensively in this area and its conclusions support the view that today's Christian is swept up in the world's view when it comes to absolutes and therefore apply this compromised attitude to non-negotiable doctrines. Existentialism that has crept into the Church has brought the Church to question:

1. The authority of the Bible
2. The inerrancy of the Bible
3. The doctrine of salvation
1. The doctrine of the deity of Christ
4. The doctrine of eternal security
5. The doctrine of eternal damnation
6. The doctrine of Christ's Second Coming

7. The doctrine of God's view toward Israel and His Jewish people
8. The doctrine of ethical and moral purity
9. The doctrine of family values.

In sharp contrast to existentialism and its basis on the existentialist's value system that centers on the individual and perhaps on disciplining oneself to accept life with its many paradoxes, biblical wisdom centers around Almighty God; it says that "the fear of the Lord is the beginning of wisdom" (Proverbs 1:7). This wisdom would guide an individual in day-to-day living. This wisdom of God as reflected through Old Testament wisdom literature provided the Jewish nation with basic common-sense morality that dictated individual conduct in many circumstances.

Clearly, if one chooses the sleeping pill of existentialism, they will have a nightmarish life.

The Pluralism And Relativism Pills

Religious pluralism teaches that no single religion can claim absolute authority to teach absolute truth. The worldview is that one's religion is not the sole and exclusive source of truth. Further, a distinction exists between what may be claimed as literal in a religious text and what may be metaphorical. The text, therefore, is open to interpretation. Accordingly, no one religion is able to comprehensively capture and communicate all truth. Because of the finite and fallible nature of human beings, no text written by man can truthfully describe God's will, counsel, or plan of salvation, since it is God apart from man who reveals divine thoughts and plans. This philosophy has created the following enigma:

> Many people hold that it is both permissible and imperative for people of all faiths to develop some form of religious pluralism. They believe that it is intellectually valid to do so because since Biblical times, humanity's understanding of man's place in the natural world has changed radically, due to advances in science; since Biblical times, philosophers have challenged humanity to rethink the notion of truth...[84]

What has been established is that there is no way of determining any biblical standard or absolute, but that since all religions have a common denominator (that being a "god"), then we can accept the thinking that there are many different ways to God, none of which have the "real" truth. This idea has presented modern day philosophers with the task to rethink the notion of truth.

Akin to pluralism is relativism. This teaching holds that all religions are equal in value and that none of the religions gives access to absolute truth—that truth varies from person to person, culture to culture, and time to time—freeing people from the tyranny of absolutes. This in its very character smacks of syncretism—the blending of beliefs, creeds, and practices from different religions into one mutual faith. This belief has led to:

> In recent years, some Christian groups have become

more open to religious pluralism; this has led to many cases of reconciliation between Christians and people of other faiths. This liberalization of the majority of seminaries and theological institutions, particularly in regards to *the rejection of the notion that the Bible is a divinely authored document*, has facilitated a much more human-centered and secular movement within mainstream Christian denominations, particularly in the United States. Most mainstream churches no longer hold to exclusive view on salvation (emphasis added).[85]

Arguing against this belief, the Christian view is:

If Christianity is true, then other religions cannot be equally true, although they may combine some truth with their lies and errors. So the pluralist must either distort Christianity to make it pluralistic, or reject it and acknowledge that one cannot be a complete pluralist . . . Many Protestant Christian groups hold that churches which cling to certain fundamentals provide the pathway to salvation. They continue to believe in "one" church, believing in fundamental issues there is unity and non-fundamental issues there is liberty.[86]

Pluralism and relativism undermine and deny the changeless conceptual validity of God where His sovereign attributes are clearly proclaimed in the special revelation of the written Word and in the general revelation of nature (cf.

Psalm 19:1-3). Thus, God can say, "I the LORD do not change" (Malachi 3:6), along with "Jesus Christ is the same yesterday and today and forever" (Hebrews 13:8). God's immutability thus declared amidst a changing world must serve as the bedrock for society in order for there to be any standards at all. In His Word He also claims absolute authority as Sovereign LORD, demanding that no other gods be put before Him (Exodus 20:3) and maintains that one religion *can* claim absolute truth and authority, that being Fundamental Christianity with its basis of authority in the Bible. This position is arrived at through sound hermeneutics, the history of the church, relevant data, and criteria of truth attested to by the internal witness of the Holy Spirit to the teaching of the Word of God. This is exhibited in the following passages:

1. I am the LORD and there is no other. I, the LORD, speak the truth; I declare what is right (Isaiah 45:19).

2. I am the way and the truth and the life. No one comes to the Father except through me (John 14:6).

If there is to be any truth in society, there must be a standard to measure un-truth's by. When Christ was before Pilate, he asserted that He had come to testify of truth. The personification of Truth stood before him, yet, Pilate in turn asked him, "What is Truth?" (John 18:38). This is the same question that is being asked today by the pluralist and the relativist: "What is truth?" Using the argument that

Scripture is not absolute truth because it was written and interpreted by man is a direct contradiction of Truth:

> 1. All Scripture is God-breathed ("inspired") and is useful for teaching, rebuking, correcting and training in righteousness (2 Timothy 3:16).
> 2. . . . men spoke from God as they were carried along by the Holy Spirit (2 Peter 1:21).

The doctrine of Inerrancy declares that the inspired Word of God, the Bible, is without error (in the original manuscripts). While there may be copyist errors in the transmission of the Bible through the ages, no errors exist in the fundamental doctrines.

The philosophy of men that has led to the pluralism and relativism pill is rebuked by the apostle Paul, "See to it that no one takes you captive through *hollow and deceptive philosophy* which depends on human traditions and the basic principles of this world rather than on Christ," (Colossians 2:8, emphasis added). He adds, "Turn away from godless chatter and the opposing ideas of what is *falsely called knowledge,* which some have professed and in so doing have wandered from the faith" (1 Timothy 6:20, emphasis added) (cf. I Corinthians 2:12-15). The philosophy of men when swallowing the pluralism and relativism pill therefore dictates that there is more than one way to God which is a direct violation of the Divine Writ, the Bible:

> 1. I, even I, am the LORD, and apart from me there is no savior (Isaiah 43:11).

2. I am the way and the truth and the life. No one comes to the Father except through me (John 14:6).

3. Salvation is found in no one else, for there is no other name under heaven given to me by which we must be saved (Acts 4:12).

The false system Paul speaks about (Romans 1:25) is the humanistic system distributing the pluralism and relativism pill which is nothing more than a placebo to cause humanity to believe that there are many roads to God and heaven, but these falsehoods are born in the cradle of lies.

The liberal notion that pluralism and relativism are impotent forces in the world of apologetics is a fallacious argument since it truly has a strong foothold in the Church and is increasingly directing Church polity. With the Emerging Church embracing pluralism and relativism, the Church is now in a perilous place because, "appeasement theology never works. It has no foundational power. It merely creates a boring compromise with the secular culture, a mishmash of beliefs that non-believers —who need no endorsement from a defunct belief system they have already rejected—could care less about."[87]

The invasion of pluralism explains why few have a passion for evangelism and why few believe in separation from the unbelieving world. Pluralism can teach that we have common ground when addressing God (that God being whoever you may choose, be it Jehovah, Allah, Vishnu, or Ra) until the time comes when one speaks about specifics. Once you enter into dialog with a pluralist about *who* your

Savior and God is, that's when the screaming and fighting begins. Any pluralist or relativist will converse with an individual when they discuss a generic, one-size-fits-all god, but mention that your God is Jesus and that He is Lord, and the conversation is over. Case in point: Islam will never surrender to any form of pluralism, relativism, or syncretism because the practice of other religions is forbidden in Saudi Arabia which possesses a national dogma of total intolerance.

But in the Christian Church, the exhortation to separation has lost its meaning when it is slumbering from the pluralism pill.

These "isms" are filling the spiritual vacuum in America because the Church has lapsed into spiritual narcolepsy. If the Church were doing its job to spread the Gospel and defend the Truth of the Bible, these "ism" pills would not be swallowed like the poisoned Kool-Aid in the Jonestown disaster. Instead, these "isms" have opened the door of spiritual America to the growing menace of Islam and other eastern religions and cults that seek to displace Fundamental Christianity.

I close this chapter with Abraham Lincoln's invocation for National Proclamation of Prayer and Repentance, circa, 1863:

> We have forgotten God. We have forgotten the gracious hand, which preserved us in peace, and multiplied and enriched and strengthened us; and have vainly imagined, in the deceitfulness of our hearts, that all these blessings were produced by

some superior wisdom and virtue of our own. Intoxicated with unbroken success, we have become too self-sufficient to feel the necessity of redeeming and preserving grace, too proud to pray to God that made us! It behooves us, then, to humble ourselves before the offended Power, to confess our national sins, and to pray for clemency and forgiveness.

Dr. Ralph D. Curtin

CHAPTER 6
Sleeping Sickness

But you-all you do is sleep. When will you wake up? "Let me sleep a little longer!" Sure, just a little more! And as you sleep, poverty creeps upon you like a robber and destroys you; want attacks you in full armor.

Proverbs 6:9-11 TLB

When the Church sought to get in bed and "sleep around" with the world, it was only a matter of time before it became dependent on "sleeping pills" to ease their seared conscience cluttered with numerous concessions that ultimately brought on a spiritual sleep disorder. This addiction to "sleeping pills" has led to a serious dose of Church "encephalitis," the dreaded "sleeping sickness" carried by the vector of the tsetse fly of compromise.

This sleeping sickness has distorted America's view of allegiance to the God who enabled our founding Fathers to pen the Constitution and build this nation. He was and still is, the God of the Bible, Jehovah, the God of Israel.

While at one time America's God was clearly designated, today, it is not. The outworking of this sleeping sickness has affected America's belief system so that its God is indefinable. Is America's God Allah? Vishnu? Brahma? Namaste? Mother Earth? *Who is the God of America?* With the brains of the Church being swollen by the bite of the bug of the world's philosophy, the Church has been unable to stave off the epidemic of encephalitis. *When will you wake up?*

Friedrich Nietzsche, the German philosopher, said, "Now it is our preference that decides against Christianity, not arguments." Despite his atheistic existentialism, his statement has merit. Both former Presidents Harry S. Truman and Dwight D. Eisenhower preferred to honor the God of the Bible while in public office. Truman said, "The fundamental basis of this nation's laws was given to Moses on the Mount. The fundamental basis of our Bill of Rights comes from the teachings . . . If we don't have the proper fundamental moral background, we will finally wind up with a totalitarian government which does not believe in rights for anybody except the state." Eisenhower added in 1953, "Almighty God ... give us, we pray, the power to discern clearly right from wrong, and allow all our words and actions to be governed thereby, and by the laws of this land."[88] Their preference defined America's God to be the God of the Bible and is what defined America as being a Christian nation. One cannot help but reflect on the "divisions" occurring in America today and how the influx of pagan religions, under our protective umbrella of "religious freedom," has caused us to turn on each other as we, as a nation, have turned away from the God of the Bible.

> **BIBLICAL WARNING**
> When a land falls into the hands of the wicked, he [God] blindfolds its judges. —Job 9:24

The sleeping sickness that America is experiencing began with the lethargy of the Supreme Court where America's highest judicial office made a command decision to forsake God by prohibiting prayer and Bible reading in public schools. Today as a substitute, young minds are being brainwashed by atheistic and pagan teachings where the very expression of the God of the Bible is banned. The following chart is an exhibit of the outworking of America's sleeping sickness:

Chronology Of Biblical Violations

For although they knew God, they neither glorified him as God nor gave thanks to him, but their thinking became futile and their foolish hearts were darkened. Although they claimed to be wise, they became fools and exchanged the glory of the immortal God for images made to look like mortal man and birds and animals and reptiles. Therefore God gave them over in the sinful desires of their hearts to sexual impurity for the degrading of their bodies with one another. They exchanged the truth of God for a lie, and worshiped and served created things rather than the Creator-who is forever praised. Amen (Romans 1:21-25).

DATE	VIOLATION
6/17/63	Supreme Court passes a law that removes prayer by forbidding the free exercise of voluntary prayer or Bible reading in public schools (Prayer in schools first forbidden on 6/25/62).
1/23/73	Legalization of abortion (Roe V. Wade).
1985	Alabama Court (11th Court of Appeals) rules against one-minute period of silence in schools "for meditation or voluntary prayer" (Contrast Oregon and Washington school officials who arranged for thousands of public school students to hear a speech delivered by Dalai Lama, a revered Buddhist religious figure (Agape Press, 5/9/01).
1992	The Supreme Court ruled that any officially-sanctioned prayer at public school graduation ceremonies violates the Establishment Clause (Lee vs. Weisman).
1997	The Supreme Court struck down the 1996 Communications Decency Act which censored the Internet by banning "indecent" speech (Reno vs. ACLU).
6/25/98	New York teacher fired for prayer in classroom while another NYC tenured teacher became a member of a national pedophile organization and was merely reassigned and given a gentle rebuke.
9/25/98	ACLU wins suit to remove Nativity scene from the front of City Hall (St. Louis, MO).
12/17/98	Religious symbols (open Bible and Cross)

	forcefully removed from Ohio City Seal; declared unconstitutional (ACLU vs. Akron).
1/1/99	California governor Davis signs into law bill AB 1001/AB 1670 that extends protection for homosexuals in schools and the workplace. They are awarded official minority status as with race and ethnicity in employment and housing.
1/13/99	Ecumenical Student Christian Ministry rejects traditional Christianity while promoting acceptance of homosexuality [Mainline denominations: United Methodist Church (UMC), the Presbyterian Church (PCUSA), the Episcopal Church, and the United Church of Christ].
2/7/99	Ohio First District Court of Appeals reversed the fifty-one-year prison sentence of a child rapist because the judge, when imposing punishment, quoted from the Bible.
10/1/99	New Jersey Supreme Court ruled that the Boy Scouts of American had violated the state's nondiscrimination law by removing a member who had publicized his homosexuality. The court ruled that such a dismissal violated New Jersey's anti-discrimination law.
12/20/99	Vermont legalizes "civil-union" that enables marriage rights for same-sex partners (Baker vs. Vermont).
5/4/00	Activists teach Massachusetts youth about homosexual sex. Using state tax dollars and hoping to skim beneath the public's radar, two pro-

homosexual activists groups gave explicit homosexual sex lessons to kids as young as fourteen, and then tried to hide their deed from parents (Culture Facts, CNSNews 5/3/00).

6/20/00   Supreme Court rules that school prayer (at sports events, etc.) is unconstitutional (Sante Fe Independent School District vs. Doe, 2000 WL 775587 U.S.).

2000   Supreme Court strikes down Nebraska's ban on partial-birth abortion (Stenberg vs. Carhart, 2000 WL 825889 (U.S.).

11/6/00   Al Gore, presidential candidate, openly supports unrestricted abortion on demand as well as public financing of abortion along with opposing the ban on partial-birth abortion.

12/26/00   California Assembly Bill #1785/1931 eliminates discriminatory attitudes and practices toward homosexuals in school curriculum.

6/28/02   California's 9th Circuit U.S. Court of Appeals rules it is unconstitutional to publicly recite the Pledge of Allegiance with the words, "Under God" (inserted in 1954).

8/5/02   California passes bill AB 1080/2651 giving same-sex partners equal benefits afforded to heterosexual spouses. Foster parents required to attend "sensitivity training" that force them to affirm sexual choices in children in their care. Homosexual couples are given priority as potential foster parents while parents with religious convictions are eliminated from the system.

2002	Broward County Schools agree to homosexual tolerance training for educators.
12/5/02	Pennsylvania governor signs pro-homosexual, anti-free speech Bill. This law could prohibit clergymen from preaching against homosexuality from the pulpit.
3/2/03	Food and Drug Admin bends its own rules and approves of the abortion pill, RU-486.
5/3/03	The body of murdered socialite, Laci Peterson, and her unborn son presents a problem for the "pro-choice" movement.
6/7/03	California Assembly passes AB 205 giving same-sex partners all rights, protection, benefits as imposed on heterosexual partners.
6/26/03	Texas Supreme Court declares sodomy laws unconstitutional. The court overruled sodomy laws it had upheld in 1986 in a Georgia case. Justice Anthony M. Kennedy wrote for the 6-3 majority that the earlier interpretation "demeans the lives of homosexual persons." Kennedy said gay men and lesbians were "entitled to respect for their private lives" and the state could not "control their destiny by making their private sexual conduct a crime" (Lawrence vs. Texas).
7/3/03	U.S. Circuit Court of Appeals (Alabama) denies Supreme Court Justice Moore's appeal to display Ten Commandments in his courtroom.
7/14/03	Bible verses are prohibited and removed from display at Grand Canyon National Park.
7/18/03	Florida Boy Scouts denied charitable funding

since they refused to permit homosexuals as Scout Leaders.

2003   Federal law allows for abortions on minor girls (eighteen yrs.) without parental consent.

8/5/03   California Gov. Davis signs Cross-dressing Bill into law. Employers can no longer prohibit cross-dressing of their employees.

8/6/03   First homosexual Episcopalian bishop voted in Episcopal denomination.

10/7/03   "F—" word permitted on TV.

11/3/03   Supreme Court rejects appeal in Alabama to exhibit Ten Commandments.

11/18/03   Massachusetts Supreme Court permits same-sex marriage.

1/13/04   New Jersey Gov. James McGreevey signs legislation conferring new financial benefits and legal rights on homosexual couples. He later declared himself a homosexual and while married, had a homosexual affair with another man.

6/30/04   Richmond, VA: Homosexuals move a step closer to ordination in the Presbyterian church after legislative committee approves a measure that would partly lift the church's ban on homosexual ministers.

7/14/04   Senate rejects move to ban same-sex marriage, paving the way for same-sex marriage to be endorsed in all fifty states.

7/14/04   Supreme Court sides with pornographers again, invalidating the Child Online Protection Act (COPA). Justice Kennedy declared it unconstitutional for Congress to stop porn flowing to teens, shifting the burden to families to screen out the graphic sex rather than imposing the cost on the companies profiting from the filth.

4/21/05 Connecticut governor M. Jodi Rell signs a law allowing civil unions for homosexual couples, becoming the first state to do so. Vermont is the other state to allow civil unions, which carry the rights and privileges of marriage without the marriage license. Massachusetts allows homosexual couples to marry.

6/27/05 The Supreme Court strikes down Ten Commandments displays in courthouses, holding that two exhibits in Kentucky crossed the line between separation of church and state because they promoted a religious message. The suit was filed by the ACLU (McCreary County v. ACLU, 03-1693).

7/20/05 Canada's Senate votes to adopt landmark legislation to legalize homosexual marriage nationwide despite fierce opposition from Conservatives and religious leaders.

9/14/05 A federal judge in California (San Francisco) declared the reciting of the Pledge of Allegiance in public schools unconstitutional. U. S. District Judge Lawrence Karlton ruled that the pledge's reference to one nation "under God" violates school children's right to be "free from a coercive requirement to affirm God." The suit was brought to the 9th U.S. Circuit Court of Appeals by atheist

Michael Newdow.

5/19/06 Louisville, KY federal judge blocks a southern Kentucky high school from including prayers in its graduation ceremony. The ACLU filed a federal lawsuit seeking a restraining order on behalf of an unidentified student at Russell County High School, ninety miles south of Louisville.

9/13/06 St. Louis, MO. South Iron Elementary School in Annapolis, MO, appealed a decision of federal Judge Catherine Perry, who issued a preliminary injunction barring the school from distributing Bibles. The lawsuit, filed by the ACLU, centered on the Gideons distributing Bibles to fifth graders.

10/26/06 Newark, NJ–New Jersey's Supreme Court issued a decision ordering the Legislature to give all the rights of marriage to same-sex couples. The Court stopped one vote shy of granting same-sex couples the right to marry, instead ruling that all the benefits of marriage must be granted to same-sex couples.

5/15/08 California's top court overturns homosexual marriage ban. In a monumental victory for the homosexual rights movement, the California Supreme Court overturned a voter-approved ban on gay marriage in a ruling that would allow same-sex couples in the nation's biggest state to get married.

5/15/08   Palm Beach Gdns. FL — Two German shepherds are put in the care of animal welfare workers as authorities investigate a Palm Beach Gardens man accused of sexually assaulting the dogs. (Note: Animal sex is not illegal in Sweden. Animal porn has increased in video rentals stores and a number of websites featuring animal pornography is surfacing. Homosexuality was decriminalized in Sweden in 1944).

6/4/08   The California Supreme Court denies the Petition for Stay and for Rehearing in the California marriage cases. The ruling states that the May 15 "same-sex marriage" decision would become final on June 16, 2008. Denying a stay in light of the certification of the Marriage Protection Act for the November ballot reveals the political agenda of a handful of judges. Judges acting as judges and not as legislators would have granted the stay.

8/20/08   California Supreme Court ruled that Christian doctors must artificially inseminate lesbians who want to be parents.

10/10/08   Connecticut Supreme Court Judicial Activists vote in favor of "Same-Sex Marriage." Connecticut thus becomes the third state high court to do so--after Massachusetts and California. Circumventing the legislative branches, the will of the people, and the constitutionally mandated process for lawmaking, the four judges ruled that the

	state cannot deny marriage license to same-sex couples.
11/10/08	California--ACLU, the National Center for Lesbian Rights, and Lambda Legal file three lawsuits to overturn the California Marriage Protection Act (Proposition 8) recently passed by 52% of California voters.
4/3/09	Iowa Supreme court legalizes same-sex marriage.
4/7/09	The Vermont Legislature votes to override Governor Jim Douglas's veto of a bill that permits same-sex couples to marry in Vermont. The state Senate voted 23-5 to override the veto and the House of Representatives voted 100-49 to override. Vermont was the first state to adopt same-sex civil unions in 2000 and is the first state to legalize same-sex marriage through the legislature.
4/30/09	U. S. House passed H.R. 1913 and elevated "actual or perceived" "sexual orientation" and "gender identity" (Hate Crimes Bill) to the same federal legal status as race. H.R. 1913 is not about stopping crime but is designed to be the stepping stone to regulate the speech of people who support family values. Bill sponsors claim that free speech activities are protected in this version of the bill, but exemptions can be overturned by courts or targeted for later removal.

Where was the Church when these laws were being proposed and ultimately enacted? Where was the Church when biblical precepts that protect society were being abandoned? Where is the outrage that is exhibited in Islam when their religious beliefs are challenged? Perhaps the answer lies in Colson's observation that confirms the Church is suffering from sleeping sickness: "In 1889 Friedrich Nietzsche told a parable. . . Neitzsche's point was not that God does not exist, but that God has become irrelevant. Men and women may assert that God exists or that He does not, but it makes little difference either way.

God is dead not because He doesn't exist, but because we live, play, procreate, govern, and die as though He doesn't."[89] The Church has compromised its doctrines, convictions, and homiletics over the decades so that the message coming from the pulpit has no clout. Society therefore acts as if He doesn't exist—or is irrelevant, or as Colson adds, God does not pose a threat to our lives: "Outwardly, we are a religious people, but inwardly our religious beliefs make no difference in how we live. We are obsessed with self; we live, raise families, govern, and die as though God does not exist, just as Nietzsche predicted a century ago. God is tolerated in the media only when He is bland enough to pose no threat."[90]

In order for the Church to be effective against the onslaught of evil, the Church must be the light and salt of society (cf. Matthew 5:13-16). Light to brighten lives darkened from sin; and light to reveal God's salvation, love, and goodness to mankind. Salt to retard the spoiling of our land by those determined to undermine divine laws and principles set down by God. But as Jim Cymbala stated in his book, *Fresh Faith*, "In too many places, the clergy have been reduced to hirelings—and they will stay popular (and employed?) if they keep giving messages the people want to hear."[91] Apparently popular pastors are preaching "soft" sermons that make people feel good—and might just as well be drowsing off or downright sleeping in the pews since the homily is non-confrontational. Undoubtedly, sermons that teach holiness and sanctification will convict people of sin and so be very unpopular.

The Frog In The Kettle

The proverbial story of the frog in the kettle that symbolizes lethargy has become the byword for the Church. Place a frog in a kettle of boiling water and it will jump out immediately because it senses its life is in peril. But place a frog in a kettle of room-temperature water and it will stay there—content—as the temperature is brought to a boil, thus cooking the frog. Likewise, the Christian community has adjusted to the rising temperature of the environment surrounding it, seemingly unaware that the boiling point of compromise is very near. The Church's inability to address the gradualism and current changes in the environment that violate Scripture has left it's stamp on society so that society no longer looks to the Church as an effective source of light and salt. A recent Barna research poll found the following:

> 1. Many Roman Catholics think they're evangelical (even if they have not made a personal commitment to Jesus Christ or experienced salvation).
> 2. One out of every four adults who call themselves evangelical is not a born-again Christian.

3. Throughout the United States, eight-four million adults call themselves evangelicals, while only eighteen million qualify using the nine-point theological test that defines the identity.[92]

Drawing a parallel to the church of Thessalonica, author Ray C. Stedman observes,

> It is a spreading miasma that has seeped into the hearts of many Christians who evidence it by giving up once-held moral standards . . . while the world grows hard and cold to spiritual matters . . . I do not understand what has happened to the Christian community in this regard. Believers who go to church regularly and profess to believe the Bible seem to be going along with the practices of the world around them, apparently unaware or unconcerned that what they are doing is unbiblical and sinful. They lie without hesitation. They don't pay their bills. They cheat on their taxes. They ignore needy people. They fail to keep appointments. They freeload shamelessly. They lose their tempers. They grow critical and caustic. They desert their mates.[93]

Well, what can be expected of the Church that has made alliances with the secular world? We can expect a major shift in biblical standards, which is exactly what is happening in America today. This is why Christ warned the Church to beware of such affiliations:

> If you belonged to the world, it would love you as its own. As it is, you do not belong to the world, but I have chosen you out of the world. That is why the world hates you (John 15:19, emphasis added).

Today's Church has lowered its standards in order to gain acceptance by the world. If this were not so, the Church would be hated and ridiculed. But when the Church poses no threat to the world, it is welcomed. Christ added in His intercessory prayer (John 17) that Christians should not be taken out of the world, but that they are not to be of the world any more than He was of the world (John 17:14). James adds, "You adulterous people, don't you know that friendship with the world is hatred toward God? Anyone who chooses to be a friend of the world becomes an enemy of God" (James 4:4).

Unless the Church wakes up and speaks out and sets the example for society, society takes the silence to mean, "It's

---

RELIGIOUS CONVICTION
Men never do evil so completely and cheerfully as when they do it from religious conviction. — Blaise Pascal, French philosopher, 1623.

OK—the Church doesn't mind—to commit homosexuality or adultery or engage in pornography."

Being vigilant to defend God's honor, being alert to watch for compromise, being awake so as to prevent the gradual erosion of biblical values is what Christ called the Church to do. Anything short of that borders on apostasy. If the Church is not united in its stand against the compromising of biblical values, then the Church cannot stand (cf. Matthew 12:25). It is my firm belief that the Church has lowered the bar of holiness and sanctification in order to "identify" with, and accommodate the world—the highest form of compromise.

Lowering The Bar

Evidence of the lowering of the bar of holiness and sanctification in the Body of Christ can be demonstrated by the image projected by Jay Bakker, the so-called "punk-rock preacher," son of the fallen '80s televangelists Jim and Tammy Faye Bakker. According to USA Weekend (January 12-14, 2007), and the www.GoodNewsFL.org publication, Jay Bakker leads his ministry from a bar in Brooklyn, is covered with tattoos and body piercings, and is noted as a "gay-affirming minister" who supports homosexual marriages. It gets better, or should we say worse.

Sexual scandals in the Church are becoming commonplace in today's society and add to the public sentiment that so-called "evangelicals" live sordid and covert lives while projecting a false image to the public. A pattern of sexual exploitation in churches that generally teach biblical truth has risen sharply over the past decade. Here are several examples:

> 1. In Homestead, PA, William Michael Altman, the senior pastor of the nondenominational Grace Christian Ministries, was hauled into court to answer a civil suit filed by a congregation member

suffering from marital troubles when the pastor told her that it was God's will that she regularly perform oral sex on him.[94]

2. In Fergus Fall, MN, a Nazarene pastor, Mervin Kelley, initiated sex with a female parishioner (who was the church pianist) who came to him suffering from clinical depression related to childhood incest. Pastor Kelley informed the female parishioner of his past sexual experiences with animals and invited her to watch as he engaged in homosexual sex. Before preaching on Sundays, he sometimes left a "gift" for her on the church piano: a tissue containing his semen.[95]

3. In 2006, the head of the National Association of Evangelicals representing 45,000 churches and thirty million Christians, Senior Pastor Ted Haggard, a married father of five and outspoken opponent of gay marriages, confessed to homosexual trysts with a homosexual prostitute in Denver covering a three-year period.[96]

4. New York, March, 2007. The Rev. R. Albert Mohler, Jr., one of the country's pre-eminent evangelical leaders and president of a Southern Baptist seminary, was quoted erroneously that a biological basis for homosexuality may be proven, and that prenatal treatment to reverse homosexual orientation would be biblically justified.[97] (This contradicts the conservative view that homosexuality is a learned behavior. Mohler's view would therefore condone pedophile, drunkenness, drug addiction, et.

al., as being inherited as well). Mohler later charged the media with totally distorting his viewpoint and made it clear that homosexual behavior is outright condemned in Scripture (visit his blog at

> **REHOBOAM GENERATION**
> We are becoming a Rehoboam Generation—ignoring the wisdom (and counsel) of our elders and splitting the kingdom. —Dr. Ronnie Floyd, pastor of the First Baptist Church of Springdale, AR

www.albertmohler.com/blog, 4/5/2007).
Contiguous to this mentality in the Church is the new wave of "sexual sermons" with its base in sexual images, innuendoes, and gospel drama—all designed to "pull" in the inquisitive minds that can be lured by sex. Highway billboards with catchy phrases and suggestive images may be generating numerous hits on a church website, but fall into the category of false advertising. These "gimmicks" project a false impression that the Church has nothing to say about salvation, holiness, separation, sanctification and the like, but has much to say about sex. Now one might argue that rather than learn about sex on the street, one would do better learning about it in the church. While that may be true to a point, historically, the Church was blessed more abundantly by God when the Church concentrated on the Gospel and getting people saved. God then took care of the sexual "hang-ups" in the marriage arena. The proper training for the Church should be to teach the right way to

conduct sexual relationships in marriage by what *not* to do.

Combining the negative images fallen pastors project with the sexual tactics being used to attract people to the church sends a very negative message today because it neutralizes and dilutes the sanctity and reverence of the Bible and Gospel message.

Preaching Fluff

Pastor Joel Osteen of Lakewood Church in Houston, Texas, is the author of the best-selling book, *Your Best Life Now*. On June 20, 2005, Osteen appeared on the Larry King Live show, during which King interviewed Osteen about his life and ministry at Lakewood. Behind the effervescent smiles that apparently diverted the curiosity of the viewer to seek some degree of depth was the fluff that pastor Osteen spewed forth. This "fluff" lacked any spiritual definition and to a great degree amounted to heresy. The following are excerpts directly from the transcripts recorded by CNN:[98]

> 1. KING: But don't you think if people don't believe as you believe (about preaching about hell and damnation), they're somehow condemned?
>
> 2. OSTEEN: You know, I think that happens in our society. But I try not to do that ... I'm for everybody ... you can live a good life no matter what's happened to you. And so I don't know. I know there is condemnation, but I don't feel that's my place.
>
> 3. AUTHOR: *The Bible makes it clear that in order to be in God's forgiveness and receive salvation, one must be regenerated in the Spirit. Outside of*

that forgiveness, hell and damnation awaits. That IS what the Bible says.

4. KING: Many evangelists feel that the church, the church itself, the religion, has failed. You share that view?

5. OSTEEN: Well, I think in a sense when you see certain things in society you would think that. But in another sense I see faith in America. Faith in the world. At an all-time high today. When I was growing up it was a big deal to have a church of 1,000. Now there're churches of 10,000. So many of them. So I think in one sense I can agree with that point. But in another sense I see a real spiritual awakening taking place.

6. AUTHOR: *If there is any truth in America coming from the pulpit, it is agreed that America is experiencing a spiritual crisis where Christianity is being rapidly replaced by humanism, secularism, materialism, Eastern religions, and Islam. If there is that "faith" Osteen is referring to, it's not in Christ. We can talk about "God" all day long to others, but when your God is defined as Jesus Christ, the conversation is over. Regarding the "10,000" member churches, these "mega-churches" are in no way an indication of the spirituality of our nation. And if there is a "spiritual awakening" occurring here in America, it is not in Christianity, but in Eastern and Islamic teachings.*

7. KING: Because we've had ministers on who said, "Your record (of deeds) don't count," you either

believe in Christ or you don't. If you believe in Christ, you are going to heaven. And if you don't, no matter what you've done in your life, you ain't."

8. OSTEEN: Yeah, I don't know. There's probably a balance between. I believe you have to know Christ. But I think that if you know Christ, if you're a believer in God, you're going to have some good works.

9. AUTHOR: *There is NO balance in between. Christ said it clearly, "I am the way, the truth, and the life, no man comes to the Father but by me" (John 14:6). Where is the "balance"? There is no room for error or margin here. It is God's way or no way. Further, Osteen's comment, ". . . if you're a believer in God," is misleading. James says, ". . . if you believe in God you are doing well, but the demons also believe in God and tremble," (James 2:19). The entire religious system believes "in God," (it has been shown that even evolutionists believe in the god of evolution, but that does not make them a Christian in biblical terms), but that is not enough. Belief in God will not give you a pass into heaven. We must have a relationship with Christ! There is no other way.*

10. KING: What if you're Jewish or Muslim; you don't accept Christ at all.

11. OSTEEN: You know, I'm very careful about saying who would and wouldn't go to heaven. I don't know...

12. KING: If you believe you have to believe in

Christ? They're wrong, aren't they?

13. OSTEEN: Well, I don't know if I believe they're wrong. I believe here's what the Bible teaches and from the Christian faith this is what I believe. But I just think that only God will judge a person's heart. I spent a lot of time in India with my father. I don't know all about their religion. But I know they love God. And I don't know. I've seen their sincerity. So I don't know...

14. AUTHOR: *In this interview with Larry King, Osteen said "I don't know" thirty-three times, and "I think," eleven times. One would think a pastor, who purports to know the Bible, would be prepared to answer some basic questions about salvation and doctrine with some degree of depth before appearing before millions of viewers. In Osteen's statements to King, he made it sound like if you love God, you go to heaven. If you're sincere, you go to heaven. Well if that's the criteria, then the Pharisees and Sadducees who loved God and were very sincere in their religion, despite the fact that they condemned Christ to the cross, would go to heaven. Now that's heresy.*

15. KING: How about issues that the church has feelings about? Abortion? Same-sex marriages?

16. OSTEEN: Yeah. You know what, Larry? I don't go there...

17. AUTHOR: *If you preach sermons where you eliminate the word, "sin," and any implication of that word, then you can bet that people will be*

made to feel comfortable and you will be very popular. The only problem is that it's apostasy.

18. KING: You don't call them (homosexuals or pro-abortionists) sinners?

19. OSTEEN: I don't.

20. KING: Is that a word (sin) you don't use?

21. OSTEEN: I don't use it. I never thought about it. But I probably don't . . . so I don't go down the road of condemning.

22. AUTHOR: *Christ never backed away from calling sin, "sin." He used it thirty-one times in all four gospels. But if you're a pastor who does not want to offend anyone, and provoke them to repent of their sin, then don't use the word. Now that's heresy.*

23. KING: You believe there's a place called heaven?

24. OSTEEN: I believe there is. Yes. You know, you've had a lot of near-death experiences and things like that. Some of that is very, to me, not that you need that as proof, but it shows you these little kids seeing the angels and things like that.

25. AUTHOR: *Biblical scholarship has determined that near-death experiences that often portray death as a corridor to a happy place where dead relatives greet you with flowers and feasts are strictly from the demonic world that creates a false reality. How any preacher can ascribe to that philosophy is a testimony to the influence of New Age and Satanic teachings.*

In Osteen's December 22, 2006, interview with Larry King, King added, "Who's the evangelical superstar who made Barbara Walter's Most Fascinating People List? . . . Who's seen in over 100 countries, and whose book sold more than four million copies? He's Joel Osteen, pastor of America's fastest growing church and he says God wants you to have it all..."

1. KING: Where do you—what's your view on homosexuality?

2. OSTEEN: Well, to me, Larry, it's not God's best. It's not you know, the scripture clearly defines that it's not—it's considered a sin. And—but you know what? There's a fine line. So is lying, so is cheating, so is have an adulterous affair.

3. AUTHOR: *Mixing lying and cheating with adultery and homosexuality is a gross misinterpretation of Scripture. In Scripture (both in Old and New Testaments), adultery and homosexuality are considered abominations, with homosexuality and adultery (in the Old Testament) being punishable by death. To lump together lying and cheating with the sins of adultery and homosexuality is typical of the poor hermeneutics employed by Osteen. While all sin is equal in God's eyes, there is different magnitudes of punishment (Luke 12:48, et. el.)*

4. KING: Do you like the idea of a civil union, where a state pronounces at least that two people get the rights of marriage?

5.OSTEEN: You know, Larry, I have not thought about that. I don't really spend much time thinking on that. I think that, you know, anything that contradicts the Bible wouldn't be something I could, you know, I could agree with.

6. AUTHOR: *Consistent with Osteen's reply is a non-committal, neutral position—one that plays well on TV and in the marketplace. Apparently Osteen does not spend much time dwelling on God's Word since homosexuality is one of the major contributors to the demise of the family. In God's dealing with mankind, He superintends His blessings, justice, and punishments through three systems of order in society: The Government which preserves order, The Church which propagates the Kingdom of God, and The Family which propagates life. For Osteen not to have convictions and address any subject that threatens the family is outright wrong for the deterioration of the family leads to the eventual collapse of the nation.*

7. KING: You don't preach much about sin. You don't talk about Satan a lot. Why?

8. OSTEEN: Well, I think I do in a sense. I don't maybe–I don't maybe–I don't know if I necessarily call it sin per se, but I'll talk about being faithful in relationships and living a life of integrity and things like that.[99]

9. AUTHOR: *If more preachers called sin "sin" and spoke out about it, then maybe we would have less of it in America. But instead, America has*

rampant violence, unprecedented drug addiction, uncontrollable sexual crimes, licensed Internet pornography, overflowing prisons, and on and on it goes. When we take the very thing Christ came to die for, "sin," off the table and preach fluff, America will continue to slide down the slippery slope to debauchery and anarchy. If there's anything that we've learned from experience, it's that we've learned nothing from experience. It's high time we put "sin" back into our vocabulary. If the public doesn't hear if from the pulpit, where will they hear it?

In this second interview, Osteen said, "I don't think," five times. "You know," fifty-six times. "I think," nineteen times and "I don't know," twenty-three times. As a spokesperson for the largest evangelical church in America, Osteen has failed miserably at apologetics and has to be the worst example of a pastor who, in front of millions of viewers, answered for the corporate Church. His interviews were riddled with fluff and not facts.

This is the kind of impotency and compromise that can be expected when the Church is suffering from spiritual sleeping sickness.

The Busy Church

Henry David Thoreau said, "It is not enough to be busy ... the question is: what are we busy about?" Today's Church is too busy to see that it has drifted away from God's plan and purpose for the Church. The Church is so busy with programs, activities, pageants, Bingo, bazaars, carnivals, televised worship, seminars, martial arts clubs and the like that the public no longer see God's house as a place of worship, but as an entertainment center. The Church has become a civic center with all kinds of social niceties. Chadwick, familiar with the problem said, "Stage-lights have found their way into the Church. The red glare dazzles, but it does not burn. Fireworks are brilliant, but they end with the hour. No ideals are kindled, no ministry impelled, no sacrifice inspired. The pretense of spirituality is the worst profanity."[100] In Chadwick's estimation, the Church has been profaned; so then, can God bless something that is profaned? In what way is the Church being blessed? According to Osteen, there is a revival of faith and that the mega-church is a sample of God's blessing, but Chadwick disagrees, and unless we see that truth, we shall continue to suffer from the sleeping sickness that has engulfed the Church.

This busyness in the Church has distracted many from dealing with important issues that pertain to laws being changed all around us that continue to restrict Christianity. Evidence of this comes from an article in the *Agape Press* entitled: "Study Finds Most U.S. Churches Fairly Uninvolved in Politics." The article states:

> Two recent studies show few churches in the United States are actively involved politically, despite many other findings in the mainstream media, a spokesman for one national research firm says. In these studies, researchers found that pastors and lay

church members generally view their congregations as largely uninvolved in politics. The studies revealed that the churches most likely to be involved politically are Pentecostal and Southern Baptist congregations ... even in those denominational groups, few churches go beyond being "somewhat involved" in national or local political issues.[101]

With few Christians being involved in politics, the non-Christians garner the majority votes from dissidents and pass laws that dishonor God.

The outworking of this sleeping sickness can be found in a "Christian" college banning several national and international Christian student organizations because the groups are too evangelical. Georgetown University, which boasts a tradition of more than 200 years of Jesuit and Catholic teachings, recently sent letters to half a dozen evangelical Christian organizations telling them they no longer are welcome. A senior legal counsel for the ADF (Alliance Defense Fund) responded: "The real interesting thing is that Georgetown tossed these groups, but left the Muslim Student Alliance and the Jewish Student Alliance intact. This Christian college is giving more religious freedom to Muslims and Jews than to Christians."[102]

As the Church busies itself with fluff, the enemies of the Cross infiltrate, undermine, and tear down the fortresses of God that once made this country great.

Repeating history?

The sleeping sickness in the Church is a mirror-image of our nation's spiritual condition, and often repeated in history. We can look to other great nations who have been bitten by the tsetse fly of compromise and experienced spiritual encephalitis, much to their detriment. Christians in Great Britain have experienced such an epidemic.

There was a time when England held that the Church was the foundation of their society. Government decision-making, cultural activities, social and moral behavior, along with family development all revolved around the nation's view toward God and sensitivity toward the Church. But as Barna states, that has all changed. "More recently these values have been undermined by the encroachment of secularism. There is more concern now for the material than for the spiritual. God is no longer at the center of the nation's agenda. Its Christian community has all but disappeared. Once representing the vast majority of that great nation's population, true believers are estimated now to be only about 2 percent of the population."[103]

Uncanny similarities exist between modern-day America and the England Barna describes. The spiritual decline of England can be easily traced back to the impotence of the Church of England's compromising theology and philosophies in the midst of a whirlpool of change and a hostile societal environment. The end game of England's snubbing its nose at God is that more than ten percent of their churches have been formally declared redundant by the Church of England. Many now serve as mosques or Sikh temples, with many more now serving as cafes, concert halls, warehouses or chic apartments. St. Paul's Church in Bristol, England, now houses a circus.

Unless the Church of America wakes up, we shall suffer the same fate.

Men to Stand In The Gap

Throughout history, God has demonstrated that He is not interested in buildings, but in men's hearts. He seeks men. He needs men to carry out His mission. Men are God's tools. The Church may be looking for better tools and methods, but God is looking for better men. He has trusted the Gospel to men. He has anointed His Spirit on men. While the Church may be looking for new methods, frills, bells, and whistles to attract people, God is looking for men to place His Holy Spirit upon. The Holy Spirit does not come upon machines or methods, but upon men. He indwells the Body of Christ, distributes its forces and empowers its members. He does not work through organizations, but through men. He is looking for men to stand in the gap between Himself and the systems of the world that continue unabated to bring Him dishonor.[104]

CHAPTER 7
The Looming Nightmare

"I've had a terrible nightmare," he said as they stood before him, "and I can't remember what it was. Tell me, for I fear some tragedy awaits me."

Daniel 2:3 TLB

While the body sleeps, the mind often continues to dictate to the human sub-conscious the events that may befall it in the future—often of nightmarish proportions. Frequently bordering on reality, looming nightmares often convey the possibility that dreaded fears and tragedies may come true. Bad dreams turn horrific when the dreamer becomes the victim who cannot escape the hands of the assassin, only to be suddenly rescued by an alarm clock before death strikes.

Babylonian King Nebuchadnezzar had a terrible nightmare that only Daniel could interpret. The nightmare foretold the future kingdoms that would emerge on earth, with the kingdom of Christ being the final and ultimate kingdom. The rise and fall of the empires on earth before God sets up His kingdom was what frightened King Nebuchadnezzar the most.

We are living in the age just prior to Christ establishing His kingdom here on earth. The signs are all around us. All the prophecies necessary for the Lord to return at the Rapture of the Church have been fulfilled. His return can happen at any time—most probably on Rosh Hashanah, the biblical feast of Trumpets (cf. I Thessalonians 4:16-18). As the world rushes to that not-too-distant day, the Church has lost its way; it is not the salt or the light Christ called it to be. As the dark nightmare unfolds, the threat of the Church capitulating to the mind set of world is all too real.

If there is no revival in the Church soon, the nightmare that will usher in the tribulation years will presently be upon us.

No Reform In America Expected

Prophetic fiction often tells in storybook fashion the horrible nightmarish events that may come upon humanity. The author of *The Left Behind* series, Tim LaHaye, has had millions of books published on the future expectations that must come upon the earth before Christ returns. His spiritual insight and prophetic credibility should act as a warning:

> Many Christians are praying for and expecting revival. While it is true that God has already given America three national revivals in the past, we desperately need another one today. Personally, I'm

> not sure we can have one without legislative reform because we have strayed so far from our biblical foundations. You cannot pollute the minds of a nation with ten billion dollars of pornographic literature annually and murder one had a half million unborn babies and have a revival. We must have legislative reform, but we [will] never have legislative reform until we elect enough leaders who are committed to that reform.[105]

Great Bible scholars and evangelicals are holding to the position that there will be no revival in America unless there is reform. That reform, I believe, must take place in the Church before it can take place in the political and social arenas. What's more, Schaeffer maintains that unless a reform that leads to revival occurs, there will be a revolution:

> The Wesley and Whitefield revivals were tremendous in calling for individual salvation, and thousands upon thousands were saved. Yet even secular historians acknowledge that it was the social results coming out of the Wesley revival that saved England from its own form of the French Revolution. *If it had not been for the Wesley revival and its social results, England would almost certainly have had its own French Revolution* (emphasis added).[106]

Decades ago, Bible scholars such as LaHaye and Schaeffer predicted that America would become a humanist nation.

They asserted that unless America underwent a revival, America would descend into the maelstrom of humanistic decadence that would lead to collapse. With the Church sound asleep—and it being the only spiritual force empowered by the Holy Spirit to prevent this catastrophe from happening—the looming nightmare of the collapse through decadence and then revolution is inevitable.

The threat of the collapse of our nation must be taken seriously by the Church if it is to be prevented.

Warnings From Great American Patriots[107]

1. Arnold Toynbee: This famous historian counted nineteen to twenty-one major civilizations that had come and gone since man began to form governments. "Ours," he said, "is only one of five which remain." He also pointed to the fact that almost all had not been overthrown by some outside aggressor, but by moral and spiritual collapse on the inside.

2. General Douglas MacArthur: "History fails to record a single precedent in which nations subject to moral decay have not passed into political and economic decline. There has been either a spiritual awakening to overcome the moral lapse, or a progressive deterioration leading to ultimate national disaster."

3. Oswald Spengler: "You are dying," he wrote in *The Decline of the West*. "I see in you all the characteristic stigmas of decay. I can prove that your great wealth and your great poverty, your capitalism and your socialism, your

wars and your revolutions, your atheism and your pessimism and your cynicism, your immorality, your broken-down marriages, your birth control, that is bleeding you from the bottom and killing off at the top in your brains—can prove to you that these are characteristic marks of dying ages of ancient states—Alexandria and Greece and neurotic Rome."

These threats and warnings come to us at a time when America's religious, political, social, ethical, and moral defenses are at its nadir. Never before has America been so vulnerable as it is now where the only force capable of turning America around, the Church, empowered by the Holy Spirit, is being muzzled. This restraint is the outworking of an impotent, sleeping Church which allows such constraints.

The future of America is in the hands of the Church.

The Future of America

Utilizing the four vehicles of mind control, education, the media, organizations, and the government, humanists and secularists have begun to tame fundamentalists (the end game is to silence the Church; often called "funny-mentalists" by the media) and stir Americans into an anti-Christian paranoia frenzy. Evidence of this plan in progress is noted by Folger, who quotes Robert Muller who is working on the anti-God, ecumenical, one-world church:

> "My dream," Muller says, "is to get a tremendous alliance between all the major religions and the UN." There's just one problem standing in the way of his

dream—those darned Christians. In *New Genesis*, Muller points out that, "Peace will only be possible through the taming of fundamentalism." The bottom line is that fundamentalism must be "tamed" to make way for tolerance. If you believe the Bible, that "taming" is aimed at you.[108]

Taming in the media is called "profiling." While homosexuals are consistently portrayed as sensitive and compassionate, conservative people of faith are typically depicted as hateful idiots or buffoons. Former Attorney General, John Ashcroft, who is true to his Christian beliefs, was falsely portrayed by leftist interest groups to be an intolerant, extremist, and bigoted man. This profiling came at the expense of violating the Constitution that mandates: "...no religious Test shall ever be required as qualification to any Office or public Trust under the United States" (Article VI).[109]

So what can we expect for the future of America?

TV moguls have cashed in on making Jesus look like a buffoon in *South Park*, a satirical show for the lower mentality of America that benefits by denigrating families, churches, and society's standards. So-called "sculptors" have displayed chocolate Jesus figures in what would be considered blasphemy three decades ago. Today it is cool. Should they have portrayed Mohammed in such a light, the producers and sculptors would not be alive today. *So what can we expect for the future of America?* Anti-Christian paranoia? Yes, most definitely.

Anti-Christian Paranoia

Anti-Christian paranoia has taken on an all-new dimension. While at one time it was considered unpopular to be a Christian, today is it considered evil. Modern authors (i.e. Sam Harris, *Letter to a Christian Nation*) contend that the suffering in America and the world is brought on by Christians—that religious hatred and religious wars are what make atheism a required belief. Other authors have warned Americans that conservative Christians are planning to take over the country. Books like Michelle Goldberg's, *Kingdom Coming: The Rise of Christian Nationalism* and Randall Blamer's, *Thy Kingdom Come*; and Kevin Phillips's *American Theocracy,* together with James Rudin's, *The Baptizing of America,* have done nothing but raise hysteria against Christianity:

> A specter is haunting America, and it is not socialism and certainly not communism. It is the specter of Americans kneeling in submission to a particular interpretation of a religion that has become an ideology, an all-encompassing way of life. It is the specter of our nation ruled by the extreme Christian right, who would make the United States a "Christian nation" where their version of God's laws supersedes all human law—including the Constitution. That, more than any other force today, is the immediate and profound threat to our republic.[110]

Dr. Ralph D. Curtin

> **WE FORGET OUR CAPACITY FOR EVIL**
> We seem to be in danger of forgetting our seemingly unlimited capacities for evil, once boundaries to certain behavior are removed. —Francis A. Schaeffer, *Whatever Happened To The Human Race?* p. 2.

According to Rudin's conspiracy theory, once Christians have reached the pinnacle of power, they will insist on Bible studies in the workplace and mandatory prayer sessions. His theory, in effect, calls for the implementation of the humanist's four-point method of mind control mentioned above (the very four that humanist's hope to control). Then they would demand the ultimate identification system for Christians who would receive special privileges in all areas of finance, education, and social entitlements while the rest of the world stood in abeyance.

Can you imagine what would happen if Rudin were to attack Islam? If he made the same allegations against, what I consider to be the real threat against America, radical Islam? But because the Church is sleeping, these authors get away with it.

When is the Church going to wake up?

Unless the Church takes a stand against the threat of amoral people being elected into office and dictating policy who are attacking the Church, the specter of America becoming a humanist nation will soon be a reality. The morals and philosophies of secular leaders are already taking a foothold in our nation. In the near future, the liberty, peace, and safety Christians now enjoy will fade into oblivion.

Should a righteous God just stand by and let this happen without taking notice or without taking action? Will a righteous and holy God take measures to correct an out-of-control society that treats His Word, His Church, and His people with contempt? Most definitely. God *will* take action.

God's Certain Judgment

The Lord is capable of raising up an enemy to humble America and with it the Church. Historically, God has used pagan nations to bring judgment against Israel in order to bring them back unto Himself. He is perfectly within His sovereign right to do so again. When the kings of Israel and Judah became powerful and their pride overpowered their dependence upon God, God raised up adversaries to draw Israel back into submission. The Babylonians, the Persians, the Greeks, and the Romans all served as God's rod of correction to teach Israel an important principle: "As long as he (the nation of Israel's king) sought the LORD, God have him success" (2 Chronicles 26:5). But when they were lifted up with pride, God brought certain judgment. This judgment is certain to fall upon the house and family of God first: "For it is time for judgment to begin with the family of God; and if it begins with us, what will the outcome be for those who do not obey the gospel of God?" (1 Peter 4:17). This is certain to be at the hands of radical Islam.

Kierkegaard gave his students the advice that theological optimism was worthless. While cock-eyed optimists today reject the concept of God's wrath, we must not forget that God's righteous love is the source of His wrath. Today's

Church has neglected to include in the homily the verses that include "wrath" as the active opposition of God's holy nature to anything that is evil. To "remove sin and God's wrath from the table" of the sermon is to assert that God does not really care about sin. History dictates otherwise: God does care about sin enough to act.

Eschatological Wrath

Having simply a cursory knowledge of the Bible will lead anyone to realize that God has acted in the past and will act in the future to defend His Word, His honor, and His Name. When we see the word wrath (Gr. *orge*) in the New Testament used over thirty-six times, with the verb forms of the cognate *orgizo* used eight times by all the Gospel writers, we can conclude that God means business when it comes to judgment.

"You brood of vipers (family of asps!), who warned you to flee from the wrath [*orge*] to come?" (Matthew 3:7). Apparently Christ also meant business when it came to judgment. Together with I Peter 4:17, this warning of permanent, long-lasting punishment by Christ to the Pharisees and Sadducees, the spiritual leaders at the time, can and must be taken as a principle that includes all those who continue to flout their sin before God. The judgment begins with the Church as Christ's light-bearers. Yes, there are other applications such as the future wrath to come upon the earth described in Matthew 24 and Revelation, and God's wrath and judgment that extends to those who reject His invitation of salvation. But we cannot dismiss the application to today's corporate Church.

Expected Punishment

The fact that America is not mentioned in Bible prophecy leads many scholars to believe that the United States falls from power and is absorbed by other nations—perhaps the European Union (EU).

Historical precedence exists in Scripture that warrants a closer look at the possibility that unless America repents, punishment can be expected. In the case of Hoshea, the last king of Israel during the divided kingdom, it was said that "he did evil in the eyes of the Lord," (2 Kings 17:2). Accordingly, God sent the Assyrians to attack Israel and put the king in prison. The Assyrians under Shalmaneser then invaded the entire land and laid siege to if for three years. Israel was defeated and exiled in Assyria. The following list of offenses against God cataloged in 2 Kings 17 is what brought on the punishment:

1. The worship of other gods (17:7)
2. Following the practices of pagan nations (17:2)
3. Committing "secret sins" (possibly of sexual content) (17:9)
4. Offering sacrifices to pagan deities (17:9-10)
5. The rejection of God's holy Word, covenants, and warnings (17:15)
6. The imitation of heathen nations (17:15)
7. The abandonment of God (17:16)

8. Worship of celestial bodies; practice of sorcery and astrology (17:16)
9. Human sacrifices (17:17)

What the king of Assyria did to worsen the punishment was to replace the exiled Israelites with peoples from Assyria. They took over the cities and dwelling places formerly inhabited by the Israelites (2 Kings 17:24). In turn these new inhabitants of Israel brought with them their own gods and set them up in their own shrines. Thus, heathen gods were worshipped in Israel's own sacred places.

Nehemiah adds that due to Israel's sins, not only were the Israelites exiled in a foreign land, but their wealth was transferred to other nations:

> But see, we are slaves today, slaves in the land you gave our forefathers so they could eat its fruit and the other good things it produces. *Because of our sins, its abundant harvest goes to the kings you have placed over us.* They rule over our bodies and our cattle as they please. We are in great distress (Nehemiah 9:36-37, emphasis added).

Due to America's sins that are even greater than those of Israel, God is systematically transferring America's wealth to the Arab-bloc nations. Staggering oil revenues have provided the Arab states with fortunes never before realized in all of recorded history. This wealth in turn is used to buy the very weapons and fund the very terrorist activities that will destroy this nation. Displacement theology, where

America's enemies are settling in our cities and towns, running for political offices, and growing roots to change our constitution and religious beliefs is all part of the punishment due America because of the sins they are committing.

Is this a punishment and judgment from God that will only worsen?

Major Causes For Judgment

<u>Primary Reason for Judgment: Wrongful Treatment of Israel</u>

Because of America's favorable support of the government of Israel, we in America are blessed. This is the outworking of the promise in Genesis 12:3 where those who bless (support) Israel will be blessed. But this treatment of Israel by America is changing rapidly as we speak.

Democratic House Speaker Nancy Pelosi violated American Government policy by visiting a terrorist-sponsoring state, Syria, in April of 2007. Despite the evidence that Syria sponsored and funded Lebanese terrorists in 2006 in their war with Israel, Pelosi insisted on a diplomatic visit. President Assad, however, considered her visit a diplomatic victory for Syria. God, however, viewed the visit as another token to curry favor with the Arabs at Israel's expense.

While it is prophetic and expected that the Arab-bloc nations, along with other nations will turn against Israel (cf. Zechariah 14:2), it is surprisingly disappointing to find *churches* go against Israel since they supposedly know God's view. However, in November of 2004, the three million-strong Presbyterian Church (U.S.A.) delegates to the PCUSA general assembly, in a meeting with twenty-four officials from the Palestinian terrorist group Hezbollah, adopted a resolution calling on the denomination to dump its share holdings in selective companies doing business with Israel.[111] Shunning Israel, either politically or financially, is dangerous business from God's perspective. Jewish groups cried "anti-Semitism," yet, leaders of the Anglican Church, which in the U.S. includes the Episcopal Church, U.S.A., followed in the PCUSA footsteps by condemning Israel and voted to side with the Palestinians. This sets a hazardous precedent when American churches violate Scripture (cf. Romans 1:16, etc.) and side with terrorist groups so as not to offend Islam.

These examples of American politicians and churches turning their backs on Israel are simply a portent of what is to come. Once again, the slogan, "We want oil, not Jews," will be America's swan song as God pours out His wrath. Historically, God has dealt severely with any nation or establishment that dishonors His promise in Genesis 12:3.

Secondary Reason For Judgment: America's Immorality

Both Old and New Testament alike take a very strong position on sexual immorality. Adultery, fornication, incest, and bestiality are treated as abominations in the sight of the Lord God with unlawful sexual relations being punishable with death (Leviticus 18:29; 20:10-16). But no sexual perversion stands out against the laws of God so much as the sin of homosexuality.

America's approval of homosexuality along with its

precarious position on Israel may very well be the catalyst that brings on God's wrath. The following scriptures make God's position on homosexuality very clear, yet in man's perversion, the truth of these verses has been challenged, questioned, and ignored by homosexual pundits who seek to crush the Bible's condemnation of the act.

1. Do not lie with a man as one lies with a woman; that is detestable (Leviticus 18:22).

2. If a man lies with a man as one lies with a woman, both of them have done what is detestable. They must be put to death; their blood will be on their own heads (Leviticus 20:13).

3. Because of this, God gave them over to shameful lusts. Even their women exchanged natural relations for unnatural ones. In the same way the men also abandoned natural relations with women and were inflamed with lust for one another. Men committed indecent acts with other men, and received in themselves the due penalty for their perversion (Romans 1:26-27).

4. Do you not know that the wicked will not inherit the kingdom of God? Do not be deceived: Neither the sexually immoral nor idolaters nor adulterers nor male prostitutes nor thieves nor the greedy nor drunkards nor slanderers nor swindlers will inherit the kingdom of God. *And that is what some of you were.* But you were washed, you were sanctified, you were justified in the name of the Lord Jesus Christ and by the Spirit of our God (I Corin-

thians 6:9-11, emphasis added). Paul adds "and that is what some of you were," as an imperative to be remembered: For the Christian, homosexuality (as well as the other sins enumerated) is *not* an ongoing activity.

Now, more than ever before in the history of America, homosexual advocates are seeking acceptance of their sexual expression using methods ranging from subtle, behind-the-scene schemes, to well-publicized legal proceedings, to brash, hostile activities (See Appendix A for Chronology of the Decline of Spiritual Values and the Infiltration of Homosexual Agenda Into American Culture and Church Life). The revolutionary homosexual movement is dedicated to rearranging our views, lifestyles, and legal system to promote their ideology. The homosexual agenda movement (LAMBDA, etc.) has become a formidable political force resolved on changing our society to receive privileges which the average American, either single or a partner in a monogamous marriage, does not have. The movement has redefined the family with the financial resources and legal clout necessary to bring it to the conclusion where outspoken protest either against the homosexual lifestyle or against the special welfare given them is considered discrimination and criminal.

Homosexual radicals continue unabated to challenge biblical doctrines by virtue of the fact that their lifestyle is now readily accepted, casting aspersions and doubts on biblical evidence. Additionally, certain denominations have ordained clergymen and women who rejected essential doctrines of Christianity such as Christ's deity and His resurrection and are now on the precipice of affirming homosexuality as biblically acceptable.

> Gay activists, feeling invincible with all of their victories, held a summit at the United Nations [in 2003], in which the next phase of their conquest of the culture's moral code was announced. One panel member, Princeton University professor Anthony Appiah called for limiting religious freedom whenever it poses a "challenge" to the homosexual agenda. This would involve criminalizing as "hate speech" religious teachings and Bible readings that brand homosexuality as sinful—a measure already on the books in Sweden and being considered in Canada.[112]

If biblical precedence prevails, before long many heterosexuals will be accosted with physical aggression.
The rebellion against God in our culture is not new. In Jim Nelson Black's book, *When Nations Die* (1994), he traces the history of civilizations, and lists the symptoms present in a culture in crisis. He argues that in the past 2,000 years, every empire, even those that seemed invincible at the height of their glory, caved into ruin. Every one of these empires had three factors in common before they fell:

> 1. Civil society devalued human life (Humanism teaches the devaluation of human life and is taught

in secular schools throughout America.).

2. The forsaking of religious belief (Current Barna polls reflect America's departure from Christian belief, morals and ethics as unprecedented.).

3. Celebrated sexual immorality (Refer to Appendix for a chronological study in the deterioration of America's sexual standards.).

Because same-sex marriage is a blasphemous counterfeit of the God-ordained institution of heterosexual marriage and the temporal manifestation of the eternal mystery of the union of Christ and His Church, God must bring judgment in order to validate His sacred Word and protect the image of His bride, the Church. Historically, any nation that flagrantly dishonored God's ordinances on sexual behavior faced consequences.

While in the military, I toured the ancient city of Pompeii in Sicily. The tour guide ushered all the military men into the remains of a brick home and then went on to point to a phallic symbol that was engraved in the headstone of the house. In my mind, the phallic symbol represented the decadent mind set of the society where they would place it in a conspicuous place without shame. God in his justice and holiness brought destruction on the entire city in A. D. 79 with the eruption of Mount Vesuvius.

If there is anything we have learned from experience, it is that we have learned nothing from experience.

Appeasement never works. It didn't work for England under Neville Chamberlain when forming a non-aggression pact with Hitler, it will not work in forming agreements with

Arab-bloc countries who want to kill Americans, and it will not work with the organizations that represent homosexuals who want to kill Christianity in America.

There must be another way to win the war.

Repentance Needed

God promised Jeremiah that if there was only *one* (who would repent and turn to Him), that He would spare the city

> **THREE-HOUR FOOTBALL GAMES**
> All over America, churchgoers chafe at Sunday morning service that runs an hour and ten minutes, but have no problem with three-hour football games on television. –Jim Cymbala, *Fresh Faith*

(Jeremiah 5:1). I believe this is God's plaintive cry to America today. The need is for sermons crying out for repentance. Ezekiel adds that the Lord is looking for those who will build the wall of righteousness and stand in the gap as intercessors to ward off the punishment that will soon be meted out to our nation unless repentance occurs (Ezekiel 22:30). When American churches decide that they will no longer compromise by entertaining goats and concentrate on feeding the sheep, we will see less "couch potato" Christians and more "meat-and-e" Christians. The "cafeteria-style" worship where pastors "hang out" in jeans with holes in them along with their shirt tails flopping in the breeze while they dish out potpourri sermons that tickle the ear need to yield to godly worship with reverence and respect for God's house and His Word. Maybe then God will raise up godly men and women with a passion to bring about reform and revival.

CHAPTER 8
Waking the Sleeping Church

This is all the more urgent, for you know how late it is; time is running out. Wake up, for our salvation is nearer now than when we first believed.

Romans 13:11 NLT.

It was a time, not much unlike our time, when Ahab, the wicked king of Israel, accused Elijah of causing Israel's troubles. Drought, famine, loss of livestock and crops—a national crisis. It was a time, not much unlike our time, when the spiritual leadership of Israel committed abomination after abomination, including the promoting of idolatry by worshipping Asherah poles—never looking at themselves as the cause, but blaming Elijah for the nation's disasters. It was a time, not much unlike our time, when the people of Israel followed after the wicked leadership to a place called Mount Carmel where God would proclaim who was the true God. A place of contest between the forces of good and the forces of evil. The god who answered by fire would be worshipped as God would be identified here.

Dr. Ralph D. Curtin

At Mount Carmel, the false god Baal was humiliated for his failure to perform under fire as Elijah demanded that Baal be awakened from sleep because he was unable to perform his duties as a god. He was unable to produce the fire to consume the sacrifice. Elijah then prayed, "Answer me, O LORD, answer me, so these people will know that you, O LORD, are God, and that you are turning their hearts back again. Then the fire of the Lord fell and burned up the sacrifice, the wood, the stones and the soil, and also licked up the water in the trench. When all the people saw this, they fell prostrate and cried, 'The LORD—he is God! The LORD—he is God!'" (I Kings 18:37-39).

This contest brought reform throughout Israel, but not without a price. After the wicked priests were vanquished, Elijah became a hunted man. It is not popular to embarrass or humiliate the god of the land who is not God. It was a time, not much unlike our time, when Elijah felt alone in his battle against the times when evil seems to rule. It was a time, not much unlike our time, when the voices of Christian warriors are being silenced by special interest groups and their power-broker lawyers who seem to command the courts of the land.

Yet, this is a time, not much unlike that time, when God is saying to the disheartened Christians who battle against the onslaught of evil, as he did to Elijah, "I reserve seven thousand in Israel—all whose knees have not bowed down to Baal and all whose mouths have not kissed him," (I Kings 19:18).

It is to that seven thousand in the Church today that the cry to awaken the sleeping church at a time of peril is given. It is time for the seven thousand to wake up.

Waking the Sleeping Giant

Historians have alleged that Japanese Admiral Isoroku Yamamoto, directly after his attack on Pearl Harbor, said about America, "I fear all we have done is to awaken a

---

THE SPIRIT OF WAR

The Church of Christ is continually represented under the figure of an army; yet its Captain is the Prince of Peace; its object is the establishment of peace, and its soldiers are men of a peaceful disposition. The spirit of war is at the extremely opposite point to the spirit of the gospel.

Yet nevertheless, the church on earth has, and until the second advent must be, the church militant, the church armed, the church warring, the church conquering. And how is this?

It is in the very order of things that so it must be. Truth could not be truth in this world if it were not a warring thing, and we should at once suspect that it were not true if error were friends with it. The spotless purity of truth must always be at war with the blackness of heresy and lies. —C. H. Spurgeon, *The Metropolitan Tabernacle Pulpit*, vol. 5 (London: Passmore & Alabaster, 1879), p. 41.

---

sleeping giant and fill him with a terrible resolve." That ominous prediction came true when America awoke from its slumbering isolation and joined in the war to defeat the axis powers bent on destroying democracy.

Today, the sleeping giant is not America, but the Church. The Church must be awakened in order to defeat the enemy bent on destroying the divinely ordained custodian of faith and truth—the Church. As J. Campbell White has said when considering the unification of forces: The four things that bind men together: (1) Common hope (2) Common work (3) Deliverance from common peril (4) Loyalty to a common friend. These elements must be found in the Church if it is to survive the attacks marshaled against it. The "seven thousand" who have not bowed the knee to postmodernism, humanism, secularism, ecumenism, and all the other "isms" must be galvanized in order to cut down the "Asherah poles" that are being erected in the Church today. We have a common hope: The soon return of Christ. We have a common work: To keep the Bride of Christ as pure as possible as we await His return. We have a common peril: The relentless attacks against the sleeping Church.

We *do not* have the common loyalty in the Church that is needed to win the war. Not yet.

As long as the Church sleeps at the post, disunity abounds and the war cannot be won. John MacArthur adds, "The idea of actually fighting for doctrinal truth is the furthest thing from most churchgoer's thoughts. . . they are so obsessed with making the church seem 'cool' to unbelievers that they can't be bothered with questions about whether another person's doctrine is sound or not."[113] While the "cool" ones banter back and forth about trivial issues, the enemy is digging in, planning, plotting, and maneuvering. His goal is to neutralize the Church so that it is ineffective in its fight to win souls to Christ. In his arsenal are new weapons that catch the Church unaware, yet entrap just the same—weapons such as "fearism" or "phobiaism," and "sedentaryism." These new "isms" are like a lullaby to the Church so that it slumbers in complacency.

The media cannot survive unless it continues to bring new fears into the lives of Americans. There is the danger of an Ecoli and bird flu epidemic. There is the peril of global warming. There is the constant fear of radical Islamic terrorists. There is the fear of school shootings. There is the fear of church scandals. There is the gas shortage crisis. There is the fear of contamination of pet food—and on and on it goes. All of these fears bring the nation to the state of fear where the citizen develops all kinds of phobias, whether they are real or imagined, there is the constant reminder that we live in a chaotic world where no one can be trusted and no place is safe. The end result is "sedentaryism," the condition were Americans just sit in front of their plasma TVs, eat junk food, and watch the world go by in the sanctity of their own supposed fortress.

And the Church has bought into these "isms" big time where they have grown lazy, worldly, and self-satisfied and grossly apathetic about doctrine and truth—sitting in the pew, watching it all happen.

Time to Wake Up

The wake-up call to the Church is echoed in Bob Dylan's song, "When You Gonna Wake Up,"[114] where he sings,

> Adulterers in churches and pornography in the schools

> You got gangsters in power and lawbreakers making rules
> When you gonna wake up,
> When you gonna wake up,
> When you gonna wake up
> And strengthen the things that remain?

The refrain in Dylan's song must start out as the reveille, then become the marching orders for the Church. The time has come to set aside the "fast food" diet of the world's "burger joints" that are not healthy and eat military style in preparation for battle. MacArthur strengthens this position where he teaches:

> This is a battle we cannot wage effectively if we always try to come across to the world as merely nice, nonchalant, docile, agreeable, and fun-loving people. We must not take our cues from people who are perfectly happy to compromise the truth wherever possible "for harmony's sake." Friendly dialogue may sound affable and pleasant. But neither Christ nor the apostle ever confronted serious, soul-destroying error by building collegial relationships with false teachers . . . it is our bounden duty to contend earnestly for the faith.[115]

In order for the Church to awaken—perhaps "The Third Awakening"— confrontation must take place. A modern reformation or awakening is greatly needed. We cannot set aside confrontation simply because discernment or distinguishing between God's principles and the world's principles is difficult. We must act.

Preparing For the Third Awakening

The possibility of a modern reformation or "Third Awakening" depends solely on the operation of the Holy Spirit. Holding to the truth that the Holy Spirit indwells the Christian who has been regenerated, we can expect that the Lord will use the true Christian Church to bring about this Third Awakening. But is there something holding the Church back from bringing on a revival? Yes, I believe there is. It's repentance. There is a necessary repentance of believers as well as of sinners. The believers are not transgressors of Moses's Law, but committing sins of the Spirit. As long as the Church is disobedient to God's will, as long as things that dishonor Him are not surrendered to the authority of Christ, there is sin in the camp and there can be no awakening. We do not need more of the Spirit; the Spirit needs more of us.

We need to check to see if indeed regeneration has taken place. This act of God must begin with the pastors of the Church and work its way down to the person in the pew. Titus 3:5 demands that regeneration or rebirth take place at salvation. But how many "professing Christians" have never been regenerated in the Spirit? This, I believe, is the problem. When genuine regeneration takes place, a changed life is the result. Passions for God's Word and the lost fill the new believer. Without these telltale signs, I seriously doubt the person's salvation. When we are sure that regeneration has taken place in the pulpit and in the pew, we can move forward in kingdom business. Without regeneration—the empowerment of the Holy Spirit—an awakening is impossible.

Repentance, to change one's mind toward sin, is the imperative that preachers of yesteryear demanded. Anything less than that to effect change is an exercise in futility. Charles Finney (1792-1875), the lawyer turned evangelist, insisted: ". . . as long as an audience kept looking at him while he preached, he knew he was failing. Only when their heads began to drop in deep conviction of sin did he know that God was working alongside him, producing a heart change inside. The words of doctrine alone were not enough."[116]

This conviction of sin Finney refers to is all part of repentance that follows the act of regeneration. When Church leaders themselves discover what their true relationship with Christ really is, they will hold to that conviction and bring about change. We cannot expect the man in the pew to discover where he is in Christ unless it starts at the top. Church leaders must lead by example in the area of personal salvation; then we can expect church reform that will in turn reach out into the surrounding population. Bill Bright, former founder of the worldwide evangelistic organization Campus Crusade for Christ, made it clear where the responsibility for America's spiritual problems emanated from:

> The sad state of America's churches is one of the great scandals of Christian history, and American Christians must repent, live in the power of God's Spirit and pray for revival. One of the great scandals

of the centuries is the condition of the church of Christ in America today. That revival will only come, however, when Christians surrender to the lordship of Jesus Christ, confess the sins that hinder God's spirit and live every moment in the power of the Holy Spirit.[117]

The Church cannot skip the "process" of regeneration and repentance and go directly to the results. The Church needs "ownership," that only comes when it sets aside its present agenda that dishonors the Lord and returns to Him. That "process," of regeneration God will take in a refining fire, and the only way for the Church to experience the "resurrection power" is for the Church to go down the path to the garden, the cross, and the grave.

Tough Talk Needed

Jim Cymbala rightly affirmed that tough talk is needed in the church. "The influence of filth and violence in people's lives will not be destroyed by polite talk."[118] Historical precedence dictates that Christ repeatedly rebuked the Pharisees for corrupting the teachings of the Bible (cf. Luke 12:1). Further, He held both the leaders—the Pharisees, the Sadducees—and the people responsible for understanding and applying Scripture. The tough talk that is needed today is for the 7000 who have not "bowed the knee to Baal" to come forward and say to the compromising Church, "Enough is enough. We will no longer tolerate the compromise, diluting, and patronizing in order to accommodate the masses who do not want to hear any messages that bring conviction of sin." Church leaders must be held accountable.

As the day of Christ's return nears, we can expect that demonic forces will ratchet-up their attacks on Scripture, and men of God may be even more susceptible to spiritual espionage—heresy and apostasy—than ever before in the history of man (cf. Matthew 24:12). The only course of action the Church has is to bring on a revival that will lead to a "Third Awakening."

Conditions Necessary For Revival

King of Judah, Josiah (640-609 B. C.), sets the biblical precedence on how to bring about revival. During a time of great apostasy he first sought the Lord by reading the Book of the Law. After reading the Word of God, he repented of his sins and pledged reform for his nation. God spoke through the prophetess Huldah and advised Josiah that destruction of the city was imminent because of their idolatry and utter disregard for God's laws. But because his heart was tender toward God he would not see his nation brought to ruin in his lifetime. Josiah then brought religious and moral reform in his nation by:

1. Reading and following the Word of God and keeping His commandments with all his heart and soul (2 Kings 23:3).
2. Showing his people their need to pledge themselves to God's Law (2 Kings 23:3).
3. Removing from the Temple of the Lord all the articles that profaned worship to the God of Israel (2 Kings 23:4).

4. Removing from the land all the pagan priests who set bad examples (2 Kings 23:5).
5. Removing the homosexual prostitutes from the Temple (2 Kings 23:7).
6. Removing all infanticide and abortion "clinics" (2 Kings 23:10).
7. Desecrating and removing the altars of the former wicked kings (2 Kings 23:12).
8. Removing all the evil prognosticators, mediums, spiritists and pagan household gods (2 Kings 23:24).
9. Fulfilling all the requirements set forth in the Scriptures for revival (2 Kings 23:24-25).
10. Celebrating the cleansing of the Temple and the land with a Passover feast (2 Kings 23:21).

Modern Application

The Christians who have not bowed their knee to Baal need to take back America from the occupying forces dedicated to its destruction. God's promise is: "When the righteous are in authority, the people rejoice: but when the wicked rule, the people mourn," (Proverbs 29:2 KJV). Whether Americans acknowledge it or not, the fact remains that America *is* mourning. The evidence of America massacring life is piling up all around us. That evidence bears witness to America's mourning. The national massacre of abortion. The national massacre of school shootings. The national massacre of the war in the mid-East. The massacre of the innocents defiled by pedophiles. The massacre of the innocent young minds of those exposed to pornography. The massacre of the innocent drawn into the web of homosexuality. The massacre of the innocent sucked into drug abuse. And on it goes without remedy...

The American Church must make the application of Josiah's formula for revival and introduce it into our nation if there is to be any hope of salvaging our nation from the spiritual vultures that continue to circle our dying nation, waiting to pick our bones. Applying Josiah's principles would mean:

> 1. The Church must regard the Scriptures as inspired and inerrant. Following the mandates of both principle and promise must be strictly adhered to. No more manipulating in order to accommodate special interest groups (Deut. 4:1-2; 2 Tim. 3:16; 2 Peter 1:21).
>
> 2. Church leaders must follow biblical mandates and show by example their pledge to carry them out (2 Cor. 2:15; 3:2; 9:13; 1 Peter 2:12).
>
> 3. The Church must remove from the sanctuary those programs and devices that embellish on emotionalism and busyness and pledge themselves to return to the practice of true worship before the Lord. Instead of today's Church being a place of sanctity and holiness, it has become a marketplace or house of merchandise (Ex. 23:24; Isa. 1:16; Mk. 11:15-18; 2 Cor. 7:1).
>
> 4. The Church must stand up and insist on both ecclesiastical and legislative action against those in spiritual and civic leadership, the media, and the

corporate world who set bad examples by promoting paganism and the worship of false gods and religions (Ex. 23:24-26; Deut. 12:31; I Cor. 10:14-22).

5. The Church must provide a united front in legally and spiritually combating the aggressive homosexual movement that seeks to nationalize their sin of sexual perversion. Both Old and New Testaments condemn the practice (Lev. 18:22-29; 20:13; Deut. 22:5; Jges. 20:13; Rom. 1:26-27; I Cor. 6:9, 18).

6. The Church must stand against the modern-day slaughter of the innocents and enforce legislation to rid the land of the abortion clinics, the organizations that fund them, and the culprits that profit by the abominable act (Ex. 20:13; Lev. 18:21; Ps. 106:38; Prov. 24:11-12; 31:8; Jer. 7:31; 31:15).

7. The Church must not commemorate or memorialize those spiritual leaders and their ministries that did not honor the Lord in their lives or ministry. Discipline and ostracization must follow in order for the Church to respect and honor the Lord instead of men. Spiritual leaders must be chosen from the "7000" that have not bowed the knee to Baal (Deut. 19:19b-20; John 13:15; I Tim. 4:12; Titus 2:7).

8. The Church must not engage or encourage Americans to have any dealings with those mediums that practice divination, witchcraft, necromancy, astrology, or participate with any agent who foretells the future. It is an abomination to the Lord (Deut. 18:9-13).

9. Obedience is key. Once the Church is obedi-

ent to fulfill the requirements set forth in Scripture according to 2 Chronicles 7:14...

10. The Church can celebrate the cleansing of the land, and then the Lord will shower His blessings on our nation (Deut. 28:1-14).

Regaining the Fear of the Lord

> **ABRAHAM LINCOLN: FEAR THE LORD**
> "It is fit and becoming in all people and at all times to acknowledge and revere the supreme government of God; to bow in humble submission to his chastisements; to confess and deplore their sins and transgressions, in the full conviction that 'the fear of the Lord is the beginning of wisdom;' to pray with all fervency and contrition for pardon of their past offenses and for a blessing upon present and prospective action." — Abraham Lincoln (1809-1865)

The conditions necessary for revival must be accompanied by the fear of the Lord that is conspicuously absent in the Church and in America today. Of all the phobias America is currently experiencing—the one that marks a revival—the fear of the Lord, is blatantly missing. Today, there is no fear of God in American life nor do America's enemies fear the God of the Americans. This is further proof of America's departure from God and its inherent penalty is quite apparent.

Jesus said, "But I will show you whom you should fear: Fear him [God] who, after the killing of the body, has power to throw you into hell. Yes, I tell you, fear him" (Luke 12:5).

Having a healthy fear of the Lord has historically provided divine restraint that kept Israel and the Church in line with God. Having a fear of the Lord is also a major deterrent to evil (cf. Proverbs 14:16). The nation of Israel obeyed God's laws for fear of divine retribution and in turn treated their fellow man accordingly. The nation was blessed, given divine protection, and crime was at a minimum.

When Israel had a healthy fear of the Lord, its enemies feared the God of the Israelites and would not dare come up against them for fear of reprisals—not from the Israelites—but from the God the Israelites served (cf. Joshua 2:9-11). This was a divine principle that when obeyed, afforded Israel the best form of insurance protection against any enemies that could be imagined. Here are the highlights of God's policy:

> 1. I will send my terror ahead of you and throw into confusion every nation you encounter. I will make all your enemies turn their backs and run (Exodus 23:27).
>
> 2. No man will be able to stand against you. The LORD your God, as he promised you, will put the terror and fear of you on the whole land, wherever you go (Deuteronomy 11:25).
>
> 3. The LORD will grant that the enemies who rise up against you will be defeated before you. They will come at you from one direction but flee from you in seven (Deuteronomy 28:7).
>
> 4. No one will be able to stand up against you all the days of your life. As I was with Moses, so I will be

with you; I will never leave you nor forsake you (Joshua 1:5).

Worried about the Islamic terror threat? You should be. Worried about our nation being under divine chastisement? You should be. Worried about the collapse of America's moral fiber? You should be. Divine principles found in Scripture (Deuteronomy 28, etc.) clearly warn any nation that flagrantly disobeys God's laws that judgment will come. His warning extends to the Church, in fact, judgment begins in the house of God (I Peter 4:17). Because of this truth, God expects the Church to live up to its responsibility.

Responsibilities of Today's Church

> **REGAINING AMERICA'S GREATNESS**
> If America is ever to regain her greatness, the churches of America must once again preach an authentic gospel—the gospel of free grace and biblical discipleship—not the gospel of works and superficial religiosity. Man must be told that he is a sinner, and he must also be told that Jesus is his only hope of redemption, two simple truths that are lost on most Americans, including many so-called "Christians." — Gary DeMar

We live in extraordinary times that require extraordinary measures. Times when biblical doctrine and moral values are being challenged, questioned, and compromised. The Church must face up to the task that is needed to regain American's greatness and bring about the "Third Awakening." With the current advancing of postmodernism, cults, Eastern religions, and Islamic militancy dedicated to destroying Christianity; "spiritual terrorism" is threatening to destroy the corporate Church. Unless the Church unites and takes a firm stand against this attack, Christianity in America will be forced to morph into the form of an "underground church" that existed during the first century and the Communist era. Whether or not it survives will depend entirely on the sovereignty of God.

Today's Church must hear the blare of the reveille bugle and roll out of their cots of slumber, line up for muster, and be prepared for duty. The Church has been on "R & R" long enough! MacArthur observes: "In light of all the biblical commands to fight a good warfare, it is both naive and disobedient for Christians in this postmodern generation to shirk that [call to arms] duty."[119] Sound biblical doctrine must be taught, and sin must be addressed from the pulpit. MacArthur adds: "Many churches have deliberately downplayed the biblical message of God's hatred of sin, and in some cases they have carefully refrained from identifying certain politically volatile sins—such as abortion and homosexuality—as evil."[120]

The notion of today's postmodern church polity that we should dilute biblical doctrine so as to "make the world like us" is tantamount to apostasy. Luring non-Christians into the seeker-friendly church under the guise that their worldly and sinful lifestyle will not be threatened is incompatible with the Bible's teaching. John advises: "Do not love the world or anything in the world. If anyone loves the world, the love of the Father is not in him" (I John 2:15).

The Church has been called to be markedly different from the world, Satan's domain, and to imitate or give the illusion to the non-Christian that the Church will not make them "uncomfortable" in their sin when they as unbelievers are heading toward eternity in hell is biblically wrong. To uphold God's honor and the integrity of Christ's Church in a capitulating world, biblical issues that include moral values, theological truth and supernatural revelation—including biblical absolutes—cannot be compromised to accommodate the public or the seeker.

Key to the integrity of the Church is doctrine. Doctrine dictates behavior and is worth fighting for. If there are pastors or staff or members of the Church who think otherwise, they should get the boot—even a little "leaven" will contaminate the whole loaf. Further, evangelical churches carrying a majority of staff members with secular faculties that contribute to Bible illiteracy or who are opposed to sound doctrine being taught should step down or be dismissed and replaced with those who place the utmost value on theological issues.

Once the house of the Lord has been cleansed, the Church must confess its sin.

The Gift of Confession

While 2 Chronicles 7:14 gives us the formula for national confession, Daniel provides us with the model for national confession (Daniel 9:1-20) (See Appendix B for the full exploration and commentary on 2 Chronicles 7:14: THE PRAYER OF GOD'S PEOPLE). During Israel's captivity, Daniel studied the Scriptures and came to understand that he should pray and petition the Lord, then fast and confess his sin for himself and then for his nation. Daniel was reminded as he studied the Scriptures that the disaster that came upon his people did not bring them to repentance: "...yet *we have not sought the favor of the LORD our God by turning from our sins* and giving attention to your truth" (Daniel 9:13, emphasis added). This is exactly what the Church leaders must do today. Daniel's prayer was heard by God who sent the angel Gabriel to encourage Daniel with the great prophecy of the Seventy Weeks.

Church leaders need to set the example for the Church and the nation by waking up and confessing their sin to God before it's too late. Once this is done, we can expect God's blessing on our land.

Dr. Ralph D. Curtin

CHAPTER 9
Waking the Dead

Could you men not keep watch with me for one hour? ...Then he returned to the disciples and said to them, "Are you still sleeping and resting? Look, the hour is near . . . Rise, let us go!"

Matthew 26:40, 45-46 NIV

Christ referred to the unbelieving world as the "dead" in Matthew 8:22 when He said, ". . . Follow me, and let the dead bury their own dead." The unbeliever who is "dead" in trespass and sin and has no spiritual ability to recognize their need for Christ as Savior without the intervention of the Holy Spirit needs to be told about the offer of salvation in Christ available to them. The task of the Church is to do just that: *Wake the dead.*

1. The Motive

The Great Commission in Matthew 28:19-20 is Christ's charge to wake the dead. This should be our motive as a body of believers. But if the Church is slumbering—still sleeping and resting—who will do it? In the providence of God, who knows if He will not use Iran's Ahmadinejad to push the "atomic button" and usher in the Tribulation period? With that real possibility in mind along with countless other end-time indicators, do we really have much time left to spend on trivial programs? No! As Dawson Trotman, founder of the Navigators once said, "The greatest time wasted is the time getting started." The Church needs to reach unbelievers ASAP—there is no time to waste. Let's get started!

Christ exhorted the Church to be both vigilant and prepared for the increase of wickedness and departure from the faith that will occur near the time of His return when He said, "Because of the *increase of wickedness, the love of most will grow cold*, but he who stands firm to the end will be saved," and ". . . when the Son of Man returns, *will he find faith* on the earth?" (Matthew 24:12; Luke 18:8, emphasis added). The evidence of this happening now is consonant with what we see on nightly TV newscasts. To the one who disagrees, there is blindness or denial to blame.

Can you imagine the furor and fire that would ensue if Mohammed was depicted as a homosexual? Can you imagine what frenzy would unfold against the Michael Moore's of Hollywood if Allah or Mohammed's name were used in vain as Christ's name is used in films? Yet, the blasphemous play, *Corpus Christi*, that depicts Jesus as a homosexual who has sex with his disciples slips under the radar in Christendom.[121]

> **ABORTION CONSIDERED MURDER**
> Knowing biblical values, people view human life as unique—to be protected and loved—because each individual is created in the image of God. This stands in great contrast, for example to Roman culture. The Roman world practiced both abortion and infanticide, while Christian societies have considered abortion and infanticide to be murder. —Francis A. Schaeffer, *Whatever Happened To The Human Race?*, p. 4.

Be warned: The longer the Church waits to be proactive in waking the dead, the more advanced will be the deterioration of spiritual, ethical, and moral absolutes.

If medical professionals can violate the Oath of Hippocrates that states, "...I will not give to a woman an instrument to produce abortion when performing abortions," then what can we expect from a society claiming to be "Christian," who has not demanded the repeal of the law that gives them license? In the mind of God, the concept of abortion was so horrendous that in the Law of Moses there is no mention of abortion legislation. It was so unthinkable that an Israelite woman should desire an abortion that there was no need to cite that in the criminal code. Legalized abortion and homosexual rights are the tell-tale signs of a society that has abandoned moral absolutes. And so it will go down the line until all moral absolutes have been eliminated from our society—that is—unless the Church wakes the dead.

The Case For Moral Absolutes

With the onslaught of post-modernism in America comes the relaxing—on the verge of abandonment—of moral absolutes that has cast its spell upon the Church. As the Church sleeps, society allows a woman in Florida to hire an abortionist to terminate the life inside her, but she is charged with "child abuse" if she uses crack while pregnant. A Florida school nurse cannot dispense an aspirin to a child without written permission from the parents, but a pregnant girl in the same school can get an abortion without notifying her parents.

The rejection of moral absolutes alone has resulted in sexual addiction, incurable diseases, unwanted pregnancies, betrayal of trusts, broken marriages, confusion of gender, loss of health, and death. This insane inconsistency goes on every day in America while the Church swallows the relativism sleeping pill. According to a 1994 Barna Research study, sixty-two percent of those who called themselves born-again Christians (this grouping included religious leaders and lay people) said they doubted the existence of absolute truth. This equates to Church leaders being as open-minded as the rest of the culture—being open to anything except historic Christian doctrine.

The Bible has a great deal to say about social justice, the sacredness of marriage, the qualities of a good home, and the standards of sexual morality. These absolute truths must be taught in the Church! While the Church cannot take a political platform, the individual church-goer as an American citizen can by their own example promote morality and justice in their community because we are the salt of the earth that keeps the world from spoiling (cf.

Matthew 5:13). When Christians sleep, the world goes haywire. When Christians live for themselves instead of the way God wants them to live, tremendous evil is permitted to flourish. Since the Spirit-indwelt church is the restraining force against assiduous evil, the Church must see the Bible as the plumb line of absolute values to measure right and wrong. In turn they must exemplify these values in their everyday lives.

While the solution to society's burgeoning problems is not going to be achieved through legislation that outlaws all abortions or imprisons homosexuals, these people do need to know that there is a God who hates sin and stubborn moral independence. This same God wants them to know that He loves them enough to care that they have ignored His teachings on moral absolutes.

When the Church obeys God, the Church will wield the influence needed to wake the dead.

Serious Christians who believe in moral absolutes are obedient Christians and these serious and obedient Christians are exactly what is needed to wake the dead. Colson observes: "Lenin particularly hated seriously committed Christians. Weak Christians he could manage, but serious Christians meant nothing but trouble for a Marxist-Leninist regime."[122] MacArthur adds: "We cannot afford to be apathetic about the truth God has put in our trust. It is our duty to guard, proclaim, and pass that truth on to the next generation (1 Timothy 6:20-21). We who love Christ and believe the truth embodied in His teaching must awaken to the reality of the battle that is raging all around us."[123]

With the Church heeding the call to invoke spiritual, moral, and ethical absolutes, we will not have to fear the villain of apostasy that lurks within the body of Christ. The Church will recover from its era of apathy toward false doctrine and turn its attention, energy, and resources to the winning of souls who are "dead."

2. THE MECHANISM

The promise made by the Lord to Zerubbabel is a promise the Church can claim: "This is the word of the LORD to Zerubbabel: 'Not by might nor by power, but by my Spirit,' says the LORD Almighty" (Zechariah 4:6). The Church is unable to bring about internal or external reform without the Holy Spirit. The task is much too great. It has to be a God-thing; God's ways are not man's ways. While we can only postulate on how this will happen, we know that God's Spirit can bring it about. God's Spirit must be the principle mechanism. Samuel Chadwick advises: "The work of God is not by might of men or by the power of men but by his Spirit. It is by him the truth convicts and converts, sanctifies and saves."[124]

Applying Victor Frankl's philosophy for survival to the

COURAGE VS. LOSING

We lost because we told ourselves we lost. —Leo Tolstoy, *War and Peace.*

What a new face courage puts on everything. —Ralph Waldo Emerson

---

mechanism to wake the dead, the Church must have a

purpose and meaning for existence. To reach the "dead" for Christ *is* its purpose and meaning. The Church, empowered by the mechanism of the Holy Spirit, can get the job done. This mechanism will enable our mission and provide clear theology by which it will be accomplished. While this mission has its inherent risks, if we appropriate the power of the Holy Spirit and apply the "turtle principle" that states, "one cannot advance unless it sticks its neck out," we can do it. Perspective is everything. When we look at the challenge of reaching the dead as an opportunity and not a task, it puts a different complexion on it. Emerson wrote: "Every wall is a door." Is Jesus not the Door?

Returning To the True Gospel

For Christ's sake and with the guidance of the Holy Spirit, the Church must return to the "true" gospel of Christ as revealed in Scripture. The Holy Spirit is the driving force while the gospel of Jesus Christ proclaimed through the Church is the vehicle whereby the dead are reached. The gospel is the transforming power that brings about change in lives by converting sinners and their cultures. When combined, the Holy Spirit, the gospel, and the repentant Church form an iron-clad, formidable union that can bring about reform, if not a revival, here in America.

But do we really want a revival here in America? Really? If so, then we need to take extreme measures in an extreme society. If Charles Finney (1792-1875), the great evangelist who was the link between the First and Second Great Awakenings, was alive, he would preach as follows:

1. He would appeal by name to sinners while preaching in order to drive home the need for personal repentance and salvation.

2. He would address the possibility, even the necessity, of totally eradicating sin both in the individual and in society.

3. He would stress the urgent need for the Church to return to holiness and purity as an example to the unbelieving world.

4. He would preach the gospel in the power of the Holy Spirit, without special effects and sensationalism.

5. He would emphasize the great need for the baptism in the Holy Spirit; methods to be used in the quest for souls, instructions to new converts; and how to grow in grace.[125]

Finney's philosophy of ministry may seem harsh today, but the fact remains that he did get results in his era. Over half a million people were converted through his ministry in an age where there were no "theatrical enhancements" available in the church. No, it was straight, honest-to-God preaching imbued with the Holy Spirit. Very few returned to their old way of life after conversion. If sin was rampant, then Finney would meet the challenge head-on with whatever force was necessary to get the job done. He adds, "Revival is no more a miracle than a crop of wheat. Revival comes from heaven when heroic souls enter the conflict determined to win or die—or if need be, to win and die! The kingdom of heaven suffers violence and the violent take it by force" (Matthew 11:12).

We live in a violent world today. A world of violent crime, violent sexual acts perpetrated against innocent children, and violent Islamic terrorism that desire to usurp the kingdom of God. This kind of violence can only be confronted by force, not a man-made force but a supernatural one. Current statistics show that human force has been unable to curb the rise of violence in our age. This force must come from God: Not by power, but by my Spirit says the Lord (Zechariah 4:6).

3. THE MOVEMENT

It is my personal conviction that the modern church has forsaken their first love, and that this is the root cause of its modern-day troubles. As Christ instructed the church at Ephesus in Revelation: "I know your deeds, your hard work and your perseverance ... you have persevered and have endured hardships for my name, and have not grown weary, yet *I hold this against you: You have forsaken your first love*" (2:2-4, emphasis added). The departure of the church at Ephesus is a type of departure characterized in today's church and can be traced from its deviation from what I call the "basics" that Luke describes in Acts. These basics formed the building blocks of the first-century church, and since every effort in current times has failed to achieve the results in Acts, it is apparent that we need to return to those basics if the church is to make a difference in society.

It has been said that the late great football strategist, Vince Lombardi of the Green Bay Packers, called his team into the locker room for a huddle after losing to an inferior squad. Once inside, he announced that he was taking them back to the basics. He grabbed hold of a football and held it high in the air and said, "This is a football!" After vigorous re-training, the Packers went on to win three consecutive national championships.

What we can learn from this testimony is the need for the Church to return to the basics found in the Bible. In Acts 2:42, we learn what those basics are: (1) Teaching; (2) Fellowship; (3) Breaking of bread; and (4) Prayer.

> 1. TEACHING: Instructing the Church in the doctrines, promises, and principles of Scripture and then teaching the Church how to apply them is the other cornerstone of the Church (Christ being the chief Cornerstone).
>
> 2. FELLOWSHIP: Bible-centered discussions and its outworking in the lives of the churchgoer is what fellowship is all about. Too often "socialship" creeps into the church where the congregation remains focused on every subject but the Bible.
>
> 3. BREAKING OF BREAD: Sharing meals either in the church or the home with the mindset of teaching and fellowship forms a bond that is often imitated in the secular bar scene where people congregate and have a good time discussing their favorite sport.
>
> 4. PRAYER: When the church becomes a "praying church," kingdom things happen. The chemistry of teaching, fellowship, and the breaking of bread, together with prayer generates an indomitable spirit

in the life of the church. While teaching is the cornerstone, prayer is the cement that holds the church "building" together.

I believe these basics were the main ingredients that helped form the eighteenth-century Great Awakening where America's political and social cultures were greatly impacted by Christian values. The architects of the Great Awakening built and enlarged on these four basics to form the movement that changed the world at that time. If the modern Church were to implement the following ten characteristics of the revivals that took place back in the 1800s, a new movement would take place that would eclipse the Great Awakening.

    1. PRAYER: Corporate prayer is a prerequisite for outpourings of God's Spirit. Revivals were preceded by days of prayer and fasting.

    2. LEADERSHIP: God must raise up strong leaders to spearhead the movement. Jonathan Edwards was the theologian of the awakenings and his writings were a powerful influence even until the end of the following century.

    3. DOCTRINE: Revival preachers of the Great Awakening focused on the great Reformation doctrines of justification by faith and the atonement. They emphasized God's judgment and then His grace.

    4. EMOTIONALISM: The revivalists of the Great Awakening felt that their listeners' problem

was not a lack of knowledge but a need to take action. They abandoned the formality of manuscripts or notes and preached as the Spirit led.

5. MUSIC: Music, as it was in the time of King David, was an effective way to stir religious affections.

6. OPEN-AIR MEETINGS: Whitefield preached in open spaces where large crowds could gather. Wesley took the gospel message to jails, inns and ships as well as outdoors.

7. PERSECUTION: Preachers were faced with fierce opposition from hecklers, unfavorable media, and hostile audiences.

8. TESTIMONIES: Reports of revival in other places often sparked new outbreaks as lay people who had been there shared firsthand accounts of what the Holy Spirit was doing.

9. HOLY SPIRIT: The eighteenth-century revivalists expected the Spirit to manifest His presence in powerful, visible ways.

10. SOCIAL ACTION: The revivals often led to greater concern for the poor and downtrodden. Edwards taught that it was the Christian's duty to be charitable. Whitefield devoted a great deal of his energy to an orphanage he founded in Georgia.[126]

It should be noted that in this movement, the preachers followed the formula of the Great Commission that plainly stated that the Church is to GO into the world and proclaim the gospel. In the Old Testament economy, the theology was

COME. Come and see what the God of Israel is doing here in Jerusalem. But the Great Awakening was NOT characterized by drawing large crowds into cathedral-like churches with all sorts of programs, but WAS characterized by the evangelists GOING to where the crowds were and sharing their faith in a profound way.

Here is what we can expect in America's churches if they follow the example of the first-century Church that was explained in Acts following the implementation of the four basics: "And the Lord added to their number daily those who were being saved" (2:47). Yes, there would be an outpouring of God's Spirit upon the Church and people would get saved in great numbers.

> **PROVERBS ON OUR NATION**
> Righteousness exalts a nation, but sin is a disgrace to any people. –Prov. 14:34
>
> When the righteous thrive, the people rejoice; when the wicked rule, the people groan. –Prov. 29:2

> **THUCYDIDES ON MOVEMENT**
> But the bravest are surely those who have the clearest vision of what is before them, glory and danger alike, and yet notwithstanding go out to meet it. – Thucydides

Moving the Movement

We have discussed the mechanics of the movement that is

needed to wake the dead. Now, consider the implementation. Christians need to raise their voices against the atrocities that are facing our nation. The Church must cry out until change comes. From their homes, their churches, their places of business, or from their nestled table at their local coffee shop, they need to speak up until hearts are moved, laws are passed, and reform comes over our land. The list of blights on our nation includes, but is not limited to: abortion, homosexuality, pornography, prostitution, drug abuse, gambling, restricting parents rights, and last, but not least, liberalism.

While the Church may excuse away its laxity by arguing that the moral and social issues are too monstrous to combat, and that since Christ is coming back soon we should not bother to fight against these scourges in our world, one would do well to remember Paul's teaching on the matter. We are commanded to resist the devil and his evil ways and to put on the whole armor of God, that we may be able to withstand in the evil day (cf. Ephesians 6:13). If the Church through the medium of the gospel cannot bring about reform that leads to new thinking, a revision in human behavior, and transformation of the entire fabric of present-day society, then the survival of this planet is in jeopardy. There is no hope of rescuing the world from ultimate collapse.

The Church must adopt the dogged resolve that they are responsible for the fulfilling of the vision of the Great Commission which can only be carried out when the Church is obedient to God—otherwise it is an exercise in futility.

Dr. Ralph D. Curtin

> **AMERICA'S NEW CIVIL WAR**
> We are involved in nothing less than a civil war of values—a collision between two ways of life. This is not an issue of two alternatives from which to choose, but a life-and-death struggle. And one value system is going to predominate. One is going to rule the country.
> —James C. Dobson

Lambasting the Liberals

The liberals are in control. This statement can be made today because it's true. If it were not true, then ridding our land of sodomy laws that restrict the rights of Bible-believing, God-fearing pastors from preaching against these sins (Hate Crimes Bill) would not be possible. Yet, today, it's true. So how did the liberal law schools that graduate liberal lawyers, who become liberal judges, who in turn sign off on laws that promote homosexuality and abortion—how do they get away with it? Because the Church has allowed it. Lawmakers are to listen to the cries of the American people. That's their job. If the American people say "no" to changing or making new laws that protect those who defy God's laws, then the legislators must listen and act accordingly. But if the Church's voice cannot be heard above the voice of the minority interest groups that are speaking for the American people, then we have only ourselves to blame.

The Federal Marriage Amendment is the best piece of legislation to protect traditional marriage, while the Hate Crimes Bill is designed to persecute Christians and silence the voice of God that criticizes perverted sexual behavior acted out by special interest groups. The liberal courts have then decided that it is criminal to protect the traditional marriage, while at the same time it is criminal to speak out against homosexuality. Is there anybody out there who asks what is wrong with this picture?

The Church is called by God to take action to turn the tide against liberalism in favor of conservatism if America is to survive. The Church must vote out anti-Bible and anti-moral leaders and petition legislators with a dogged resolve—even to the extent of threatening impeachment where needed in order for this message to be heard. History has demonstrated that the Bible-based form of government (honoring the Ten Commandments, etc.) and Bible-based, moral society is one that receives God's blessing and endures, while any other form of rule leads to the ultimate demise of the nation. If only the judges of America would adopt Alabama's Supreme Court Chief Justice Roy Moore's view: "I will never, ever deny the God upon whom our laws in this country depend." If this were to happen, what impact would this have on American society? National revival.

Dr. Ralph D. Curtin

CHAPTER 10
Dreamland:
Reclaimed America

But everything exposed by the light becomes visible, for it is light that makes everything visible. This is why it is said: "Wake up, O sleeper, rise from the dead, and Christ will shine on you."

Ephesians 5:13-14

What can we expect if America's sleeping churches wake up—rising from the "dead," and then go on to bring America to its knees in repentance? *We can expect to live in dreamland.* The dream of every pastor for America to repent and honor God above all will finally come true. When the psalmist wrote, "Blessed is the nation whose God is the LORD" (33:12), he did so knowing that when a nation honors the Lord, they are truly blessed.

Can America become a Christian nation again?

A Brief History Lesson

Before America's moral and spiritual life became saturated with secularism, humanism, hedonism, and materialism, America was considered a Christian nation:

> In 1892 the United States Supreme Court made an exhaustive study of the supposed connection between Christianity and the government of the United States. After reviewing hundred of volumes of historical documents, the Court asserted, "These references ... add a volume of unofficial declarations to the mass of organic utterances that this is a religious people ... a Christian nation." Likewise, in 1931 Supreme Court Justice George Sutherland reviewed the 1892 decision in reference to another case and reiterated that Americans are a "Christian people." And in 1952 Justice William O. Douglas affirmed that "we are a religious people and our institutions presuppose a Supreme Being."[127]

The roots of Christian America actually go back long before 1892 when the original settlers had God's heart in mind as they came into the new world: "The Virginia Charter of 1606 which laid out the purposes for the Jamestown landing in 1607 stated the reason for the settlement, 'for the propagating of the Christian religion to such as live in darkness and utter ignorance of the true worship of Almighty God.'"[128] At that time native Indians were living in darkness, but now, it is America that is in darkness and ignorance of the true God.

When the Pilgrims landed on Plymouth Rock and carved out the Mayflower Compact, now considered the birth certificate of America, they "went to choose a place of settlement where they could express to the fullest potential of all that God has built into them for brotherhood and love and peace and justice, and offer it all up to the glory of God."[129]

Throughout this book I have attempted to chronicle the decline of America's spiritual condition and its cause: the sleeping Church. Once the sleeping Church awakens, we can expect a Third Awakening that will have a dramatic effect on our nation. Will we be able to call America a Christian nation that has the connotation that all of America is made up of born-again Christians? No. But we can trust that God will honor our nation when we put Him first in every area of life.

Dreamland will become a reality when our governmental law once again is based on the respect and reverence for God's Word that was the basis of America's foundation. Dreamland will become a reality when the Ten Commandments are reinstated as the basis for our Constitution and civil laws and in turn realizing that man was God's special creation.

Dreamland will become a reality when the Church and its Christians stand up and say, "No More!" to the nemesis of the "isms" that we embrace.

Dreamland will become a reality when we forsake what Francis Schaeffer would call a "Christian memory," where we still embrace a Judeo-Christian value system but few operate on the basis that Jesus was their Redeemer and few profess His deity as proclaimed in the Bible in both

Testaments.

No More Offending God in Dreamland
In Dreamland, reclaimed America will cease to offend God

> **GOD'S INSURANCE POLICY**
> If my people would but listen to me, if Israel (as well as the Church and America) would follow my ways, how quickly would I subdue their enemies and turn my hand against their foes! –Psalm 81:13-14

by attempting to remove every vestige of His presence in the very land He gave us. We will return to true worship of the God of Israel, the God of the Bible. America will strive to appoint and elect God-fearing political leaders that hold to and reflect in their lives the biblical faith of the founding fathers who crafted our Constitution and Bill of Rights (this may involve the appointment of Christian ministers to office). The sanctity of human life will be upheld in the land and in the courts while reprobate sexual lifestyles and marital infidelity will no longer be heralded and no longer threaten the God-ordained family unity.

In Dreamland, reclaimed America will cease to offend Christ's Bride, the Church. The Church will be allowed to preach the Gospel without fear of being sued by special interest groups who hold utter disdain for the truth of God's Word. In Dreamland, the Church will no longer be a "theatrical stage" where the membership will be entertained and made to "feel good," but rather will be instructed in the ways of the Lord and be convicted of the sin that nailed Christ to the cross. In Dreamland, reclaimed America will actually be involved in the implementation of the Great Commission and stay out of trouble by actively spreading the Good New of the Gospel to the world and ministering to the unfortunate since God will judge humanity by how we treat people.

In Dreamland, reclaimed America will be free from terrorism because the cowards who refuse to show themselves and claim their god instructed them to kill the innocent infidels, will know that the God of Israel and of the Bible is defending this nation and will exact due punishment upon them. The fear of our God will come upon all nations that seek both Israel and America's destruction.

In Dreamland, the reclaimed American churches will drive out those who offend Christ and Christians with profanities, obscenities, pornographic media, and Internet sites. Americans will no longer observe the double standard of allowing smut peddlers and sexual deviant purveyors from contributing monies to social causes with funds derived from the slavery of others.

From Dreaming To Acting

Anatole France, the French poet, journalist, and novelist who won the 1921 Nobel Prize for literature said, "To accomplish great things, we must dream as well as act." In America today, we must do both. We must dream of how great America can be while we work to bring the dream to reality. The mechanics of working out of this dream is explained in the following quotes:

If our country survives—and I realize that's a big IF—it will be because there is an awakening in the lives of committed Christians across our nation who finally begin to realize that it is not only their opportunity but also their absolute responsibility to be intricately involved in the political process of our country and to use that involvement to turn this nation once again to the Lord.

For much too long we have allowed our government to grow farther and farther away from the direction that God has always demanded our nation take. At the same time we have yielded the control of our country to a godless, secular humanistic philosophy that has absolutely sapped the strength and spiritual vitality America has always had. Never before in the history of Christendom have so many believers been willing to forfeit their liberty and freedom without even putting up a struggle.[130]

It is my prayer that if you looked out across America with the eye of faith and you listened with the ear of hope, you would recognize the gentle stirring, you would hear the soft rustlings, of a long-slumbering giant called the people of God awakening from their spiritual slumber. We desperately need a spiritual awakening in this country! May it begin with you, may it begin with me, may it begin with our families, and may it begin within our churches![131]

So now my question for you: Are you part of the problem or

Dr. Ralph D. Curtin

part of the solution?

APPENDIX A
Chronology of the Decline of Spiritual Values and the Infiltration of Homosexual Agenda into American Culture and Church Life

(Documentation available upon request)

PRIOR TO 2003

1. June, 1962—Public prayer is forbidden in public schools.

2. June, 1963–Supreme Court passes law completely removing prayer by forbidding free exercise of voluntary prayer or Bible reading in public schools.

3. 1980–The Ten Commandments are rejected, making it illegal for students to view copies of the Ten Commandments.

4. 1999—Cedar Grove, FL: Jerry Stephenson, founder of the Grace Institute Bible College & Seminary, claiming to be conservative, fundamental, and evangelical asserts that, "We can be gay and lesbian and still be Christians."

5. 1999–New Jersey Supreme Court orders Boy Scouts to admit homosexuals citing discrimination.

6. 1999–American Airlines, discarding previous promises to pro-family organizations has cemented its place as the nation's homosexual airline with its sponsorship of Gay.com, the largest and leading homosexual website portal.

7. 1999–Joshua Brown, 23, and Davis Carpenter, 39, are found guilty of murdering Jesse Dirkhising, 13, after binding, drugging and sodomizing him. Exercising a double standard, when compared with the murder in 1998 of Matthew Shepard, a homosexual college student, the Dirkhising murder received little media attention.

8. 2000–Homosexual advocates distribute comprehensive teaching guides and videos to elementary school children that gives teachers suggestions about classroom activities that center on dispelling gay and lesbian stereotypes. The plan is to change children's minds on the subject of homosexuality.

9. 2000–Former Boy Scout homosexual, Robert Malcomb Jr, 35, pleads guilty to 61 of 107 charges including rape, forcible oral sodomy, lewd acts with children, and bestiality. This news item received little or no attention in the media.

10. 2002–Judge Goodwin of the 9th Circuit in California ruled that children could not say the Pledge of Allegiance because it contained those "offensive" words "under God."

2003

11. Bravo/NBC *Queer Eye for the Straight Guy* premiers in which homosexuals straighten out all of the faults of heterosexual men.

12. The Red Cross is allowed to discriminate in its qualification of blood donors who are homosexu-

al.

13. Massachusetts Justice Margaret H. Marshall approves same-sex marriage claiming it is an extension of civil rights to disadvantaged groups.

14. Britney Spears and Madonna give each other an open-mouthed kiss on a MTV awards' show, underscoring how fashionable homosexual behavior had become.

15. California Gov. Gray Davis signs a domestic partner bill granting same-sex couples in California nearly all the same rights and responsibilities as heterosexual marriages.

16. New York: The Harvey Milk School, part of the public school system, is a specially funded school "designed to meet the needs of homosexual, lesbian, bisexual, transgender, and questioning youth."

17. Homosexual activists hold a summit at the UN in which they insist that the remaining laws prohibiting homosexuality be changed, including "age of consent" so that pedophiles can be considered legal.

18. Glendale Baptist Church (Nashville) hires as its associate pastor April Baker, a practicing lesbian.

19. The Supreme Court passes *Lawrence vs. Texas* declaring there is a constitutional right to homosexual sex.

20. Sen. Rick Santorum (R-Pa.) said that if the Supreme Court in a pending case says homosexual practice is constitutionally protected, "then you

have the right to bigamy, you have the right to polygamy, you have the right to incest, you have the right to adultery. You have the right to anything."

21. The NEA (National Endowment of the Arts) tells students that it was developmentally appropriate to engage in same-sex intimate relations.

2004

22. Democratic governor Howard Dean signs a bill legalizing civil unions for gays in Vermont and claims his decision was influenced by his Christian views stating, "...If God had thought homosexuality is a sin, he would not have created gay people."

23. New Jersey Governor James McGreevey (himself a declared homosexual) signs legislation to confer new financial benefits and legal rights on homosexuals.

24. New York: A billboard company rejected an advertisement submitted by a minster who responded to the Massachusetts ruling permitting homosexual marriage by declaring he is a happily married ex-homosexual.

25. Jeffrey A. Manley and Jusak Y. Bernhard, a homosexual couple, sought to consecrate their union in a Catholic church, claiming, "The reason we're doing this is to make God a part of the relationship. We are making our union with God in public. We do see it as a sacrament."

26. MTV announces its intention to forge

ahead with an all-homosexual television network that will be on all basic cable plans.

27. Former governor of Oregon, Neil Goldschmidt, admits to having had sex with a fourteen-year old girl when he was mayor of Portland. In most places that's called statutory rape, but the *Oregonian* newspaper at first chose to categorize it as adultery.

28. Under pressure from a homosexual-rights group, New York State reversed its two-year position that denied unemployment benefits to homosexuals *and* lesbians who quit their jobs to follow their partners taking new jobs out of state.

29. Opponents of homosexual marriage stepped up their rhetoric, warning state lawmakers that Massachusetts would soon see the legalization of marriages with multiple spouses if they do not overturn the Supreme Judicial Court's ruling allowing same-sex marriages.

30. Columnist Joel Belz (World Magazine, Feb. 2004) asserted, based on the overwhelming media blitz and American sentiments over the same-sex marriage debate, "I think it is already too late. It's too late because even most Americans who want to restrict 'marriage' to heterosexual couples do so for the wrong reasons. To win the marriage argument, you need either to have secular arguments that work, or a population that is ready to listen to God Himself. We've got neither, and that's why I think we've already lost the debate."

31. The threat of churches and other charitable organizations losing their tax-exempt status unless the "public interest" and extended full rights, of every conceivable kind, to homosexuals was granted surfaces in the news. "They want to change our families, our schools, our workplaces, and our churches. For until they do, they know our institutions will sit in implied judgment on their ways. It is that implied judgment they cannot tolerate"—Joel Belz (*World Magazine*, April, 2004).

32. Activism for the Federal Marriage Amendment (affirming marriage to be between one man and one woman) seems lagging as Senate backers seek supporters. Observers cite that many Americans believe that this is a "gray area" of morality that is best left without tight legal definitions.

33. Senate rejects move to ban same-sex marriage.

34. New Jersey Governor James E. McGreevey, a married father of two, resigns abruptly over homosexual affair.

2005

35. The Vatican defends its policy that there would be no crackdown on homosexual priests who are already ordained.

36. Members of the Evangelical Lutheran Church propose blessings on same-sex unions and ordaining gays who are not celibate. Rev. Robert Goldstein, a gay minister at Immanuel Evangelical

Lutheran Church in Chicago, urged delegates to remove all limits on gay leadership in the denomination.

37. The United Church of Christ (UCC) put homosexual marriages on the same par as those between a man and a woman.

38. Billboards and homosexual celebrations push for change in Utah, a Mormon-dominated state.

39. Montgomery County, Maryland, School Board approves and plans to implement a Citizens for a Responsible Curriculum that would teach that homosexuality is not a choice and that religious groups such as "fundamentalists and evangelicals" are intolerant because they teach homosexuality is wrong. High-school students would have also watched a video in which a young teacher demonstrates condom use on a cucumber and tells teens that buying condoms "isn't as scary as you might think." Parents objected and U.S. District Judge Alexander Williams agreed.

40. Pentecostal preacher, professor, and author, Judy L. Brown of the Salem, Virginia, Worship Center, admits to a lesbian relationship with fellow pastor, Ted Smart's, wife. On Aug. 25, 2003, when Mrs. Smart was out of town, Ms. Brown broke into the family's basement. She threw the switches on the fusebox, shutting off power in the house. When Mr. Smart when downstairs to investigate, the theologian, Ms. Brown, hit him on the back of the head with

a crowbar. Investigators determined that Ms. Brown had planned to kill her lover's husband, dismember his body, and dispose of it, so that she could have Mrs. Smart all to herself.

41. Kirk Kidwell in his article, "Homosexuals Flex Muscles in Washington" (Lively and Abrams, *The Pink Swastika*, 210) quotes the homosexual activist, Robert Schwab: "If [AIDS] research money is not forthcoming at a certain level by a certain date all gay males should give blood. Whatever action is required to get national attention is valid. If that includes blood terrorism, so be it."

2006

42. Colorado megachurch pastor, Paul Barnes, of Grace Chapel near Denver, resigns after telling his 2,100-member congregation that he has struggled with homosexuality since he was five years old.

43. Presbyterian leaders In Pittsburgh, PA, announced their decision to dismiss charges against a minister accused of breaking church law by presiding over the marriage of two women.

44. The 3,500-member Cathedral of Hope in Dallas, widely known as the world's largest homosexual church, joins the 1.2 million-member United Church of Christ. The UCC, a mainline denomination, has been ordaining homosexuals since the 1970s, and in 2005 it officially endorsed same-sex marriage.

45.   Newark, NJ: New Jersey's Supreme Court issues a decision ordering the Legislature to give all the rights of marriage to same-sex couples.

46.   California Senate education committee passes SB 1437, a bill requiring K-12 students to study the contributions of "people who are lesbian, gay, bisexual, or transgender, to the economic political, and social development of California." SB 1437 also prohibits textbooks, materials, or activities that "reflect adversely" on homosexuals and nix the inclusion of "any sectarian or denominational doctrine or propaganda contrary to law."

47.   Bloomington, Indiana, becomes the second city to enshrine transgenderism as a protected class along with race, gender, and sexual orientation.

48.   Soulforce, a homosexual-advocacy group that targets the "misuse of religion" to oppose homosexuality confronts nineteen colleges that forbid homosexual conduct among students. The list includes two military academies and one Mormon university. The remaining sixteen schools are private, evangelical Christian colleges. The group's mantra is "you can be gay and be a Christian."

49.   Dan Brown's *Da Vinci Code* draws on Gnostic writings and continues their traditions by making up history to create the impression that Christ's real message was feminism and sexual liberation (Gene Edward Veith. "Return of the Cainites," *World Magazine*, April 29, 2006, 22).

2007

50. Haddonfield, NJ: New Jersey governor Jon Corzine (D-NJ) signs bill legalizing civil unions to homosexuals. Conservatives, meanwhile, say the new law is another step toward the decline of the family.

51. Joint Chiefs chairman General Peter Pace is quoted as saying, "I believe homosexual acts between two individuals are immoral. I do not believe the United States is well served by a policy that says it is OK to be immoral in any way." Pace was quoted as comparing homosexual behavior with adultery, also a prosecutable offence in the military. New York Senator Hillary Clinton replied, "I don't agree with that."

52. Parents of freshmen at Chicago's Deerfield High School said students were required to attend lectures on gay sexuality and then sign a contract forbidding them to talk about it afterward. School officials threatened those who were reluctant to sign the contract. There are more than 3,000 pro-homosexual clubs in high schools nationwide.

53. Missouri State University subjects Emily Brooker to intense interrogation by hostile faculty members for refusing to follow "orders" to send a letter to the Missouri state legislature supporting adoption by those who engage in homosexual behavior. As a freshman Emily was assigned to openly display "lesbian behavior" in public and then write about her experiences. Emily was slapped with a

"Level 3 grievance" (the most serious charge possible) resulting in possible withholding of her degree and the two-and-one-half hour interrogation by the school's "ethic" committee. On behalf of Emily, the ADF (Alliance Defense Fund) filed a complaint in federal district court. The school settled—removing the grievance from Emily's record, agreed to pay her tuition for two years of graduate school, and the professor who gave the assignment was removed from his administrative duties and placed on academic leave for the rest of the semester. This watershed incident led to an internal academic investigation and a call for real reform.

... MORE BEING ADDED EACH WEEK...

APPENDIX B
The prayer of God's People
2 Chronicles 7:14

THE PRAYER
The Nation God Blesses
OF GOD'S PEOPLE
If my people, who are called by my name, will humble themselves and pray
and seek my face and turn from their wicked ways,
then will I hear from heaven and will forgive their sin
and will heal their land.
2 Chronicles 7:14 NIV

Prologue

Our nation is in alienation. We are in alienation with God. People are crying out for God to bless our land, while their hearts are far from Him. With powerful forces at work in America gaining momentum, determining in their hearts to undermine the basic biblical beliefs and principles our forefathers labored so strenuously to promote, how can God bless this country? For God to bless America amidst spiraling moral decadence would be to deny His holiness. For God to bless America while we actively defy the very foundational documents upholding godly precepts our forefathers fought so vigorously to proclaim would be to deny His character. This is just not going to happen, and anyone who believes it will is living in a world of fantasy and believing in a scheme that is diametrically opposed to God's expressed will. God must be true to His Word, the Bible, and the Bible instructs us as to how we may receive God's blessings, and clearly, America is not entitled to any blessings the way things stand at the present.

According to a recent Barna poll, the following "report card" on American sentiment toward God following the

September 11, 2001, attack gives us an idea of the pitiful spiritual state of the average citizen:

> $ Almost nine out of ten Americans say the terrorist attacks had no lasting impact on their faith, though millions of adults (roughly half of the U.S. adult population) claim to have turned to their faith to help them personally process the tragedies.
> $ Half of all adults say their church has done nothing at all to acknowledge, address or help people process the terrorist attacks.
> $ Compared to just prior to the attacks, there has been no change in personal religious activity levels such as church attendance, Bible reading, prayer, Sunday school, and small group involvement.
> $ People's religious beliefs have gone unchanged in the past year, based on the nine core beliefs we have tracked. That includes no growth in the percentage of born again adults.
> $ Adults are no more likely to believe in absolute moral truth today than they were on September 10, 2001.[1]

What has happened to the spiritual fiber of America that has left us in this state of apostasy? It has been compromised! What has happened to the patriotic American who studies documents of our heritage? Do they not see, as they come

---

[1] Barna Update: September 3, 2002.

across statements that undergird our faith-based democracy, like those of the Continental Congress, that we have deliberately misaligned ourselves from them? Consider the following excerpt:

> ... We hold these truth to be self-evident, that all men are created equal, that they are *endowed by their Creator* with certain inalienable Rights ... we therefore the Representatives of the United States of America, in General Congress, Assembled, appealing to the *Supreme Judge* of the world for the rectitude of our intentions ... and for the support of this Declaration, with a firm reliance on *the protection of Divine Providence*, we mutually pledge to each other our lives, our fortunes and our sacred honor (emphasis added).[2]

Where is the cry of outrage from patriotic Americans who cherish and value these words of our patriarchs who understood the nature of God and penned these words of gratitude to His name?

What has happened to America is typical of what has happened to every nation and empire in history that has seen fit to remove the God of the Bible from the lives of their people and purpose to live as if He does not exist. Whether it be ancient Babylon, Rome, or the Nazi regime, any nation

---

[2] The words of the Continental Congress, assembled in Philadelphia to commemorate the unveiling of the Declaration of Independence, July 4, 1776.

looking to rid the land of godly restraints will suffer dire consequences. What has happened to America is expressed by John MacArthur: "The sentiment seems to be, 'Don't tell us what to do; just bless us,' as if God were not supposed to ask anything of us. Many would prefer blessing without any conditions being imposed. Give us protection. Give us safety. Give us freedom. Give us prosperity. Just don't meddle with our morality.[3]

We, as a nation and as individuals, want to be blessed by God so that we may be free to engage in *the pursuit of happiness*. But can God bless us without compromising his divine nature? This is the question that needs to be answered alongside the prayer voiced by Jabez: "Oh, that you would bless me and enlarge my territory! Let your hand be with me, and keep me from harm so that I will be free from pain" (1 Chronicles 4:9-10).

While the prayer of Jabez is a prayer petitioning God for *blessings* and *prosperity* that can be extended to any Bible reader, the prayer of God's people found in 2 Chronicles 7:14 is a prayer of *repentance* directed at His covenant people, the nation of Israel and the people of God in His Church—not the unbelieving world.

> If my people, who called by my name, will humble themselves and pray and seek my face and turn from their wicked ways, then will I hear from heaven and will forgive their sin and will heal their land (2

---
[3] John MacArthur, *Can God Bless America?* (Nashville: WPublishing Group, 2002), 8.

Chronicles 7:14).

This prayer of repentance is desperately needed in America to avert inevitable disaster. The prayer of God's people comes to us through the pages of the Bible, not the author. Historically God has punished those who have reveled in chastening Israel and will do so again in the future. This message of warning has come to us through a formidable enemy whom God has allowed to be raised up to chastise our nation as He has in the past when using unbelieving nations to act as the rod of correction on wayward Israel.

When Israel refused to seek the Lord but continued in their rebellion while relying upon their own strength to fight the enemy, they faced renewed cataclysms until they understood the message: "But the people have not returned to him who struck them, nor have they sought the LORD Almighty" (Isaiah 9:13).

The message being broadcast loud and clear to America is that we must renew our faith in the God of the Bible and repent of the wickedness that has offended God so that He can turn our enemies away from their obsession of destroying our nation. This truth is an historic fact that our founding fathers believed in whenever our nation was assailed from without or within; believing we were under divine chastisement.

George Mason, a delegate at the Continental Congress wrote: "Every master of slaves is born a petty tyrant. They bring the judgment of heaven upon a country. As nations cannot be rewarded or punished in the next world, they must be in this. *By an inevitable chain of causes and effects,*

Providence punishes national sins by national calamities" (emphasis added).[4]

Abraham Lincoln, in his Gettysburg Address given on November 19, 1863, appeared to voice the very words used in the *Pledge of Allegiance* when he said, ". . . they [the Civil War soldiers who gave their lives] gave the last full measure of devotion that we here highly resolve that these dead shall not have died in vain—that this nation, *under God*, shall have a new birth of freedom and that government of the people, by the people, for the people, shall not perish from the earth" (emphasis added). What few patriots recall is the truth that "Lincoln believed the Civil War was a providential correction of a self-indulgent nation that had forgotten God."[5]

The prudent will take notice of God's divine offer of life or death to our nation. Life if we honor the God of the Bible, death if we dishonor Him: "See, I set before you today life and prosperity, death and destruction. For I command you today to love the LORD your God, to walk in his ways, and to keep his commands, decrees and laws; then you will live and increase, and the LORD your God will bless you in the land you are entering to possess" (Deuteronomy 30:15-16). In order for the God of the Bible to bless America, we, *God's people*, must walk in His ways.

---

[4] George Mason, delegate at the Continental Congress, quoted in Peter A. Lillback, *Freedom's Holy Light*. (Bryn Mawr, PA: The Providence Forum, 2000), 21.

[5] Peter A. Lillback, *Freedom's Holy Light*. (Bryn Mawr, PA: The Providence Forum, 2000), 24.

1
Who Are God's People?

From a biblical perspective, perhaps we are expecting the wrong people to change their behavior, to repent of their ways and return unto God in order for our country to be blessed. Could it be, however, that the God of the Bible is asking *His* people to repent? This is a question that must be answered to avoid missing out on God's favor.

So then, who are God's people?

God's People of Israel

The nation of Israel, the People of the Book, God's Chosen, *are* God's People. Israel did not do anything special to warrant this title, but received it simply because of God's love toward them and to honor the oath He made to the forefathers of this eternal nation: "For you are a people holy to the LORD your God. The LORD your God has chosen you out of all the peoples on the face of the earth to be His people, His treasured possession" (Deuteronomy 7:6).

This promise does not leave any margin for error. The Jewish people have been set apart by God to receive *at His hand*, His Law and covenant promises. We read further: "What other nation is so great as to have their gods near them the way the LORD our God is near us whenever we pray to Him? And what other nation is so great to have such righteous decrees and laws as this body of laws I am setting before you today?" (Deuteronomy 4:7-8).

These promises came to Israel with great responsibility. The responsibilities included the setting of a standard for righteousness on the earth—to set the example for the nations—as well as to be the custodians of the Bible. Paul affirmed this truth where he wrote: "What advantage is there in being a Jew. . . ? Much in every way! First of all, they have been entrusted with the very words of God" (Romans 3:1-2). Their reward for setting the example of a holy nation was the Word of God, in the form of the Torah, the Prophets, and the Writings. This reward, further, required them to watch and prepare for their coming Messiah in the person of Jesus Christ as the prophets foretold in the very Bible they were expected to cherish and obey.

God's People of the Church

In addition to God's covenant people, Israel, He has adopted the Church of Christ to be His people. Peter wrote:

> But you are a chosen people, a royal priesthood, a holy nation, a people belonging to God, that you may declare the praises of Him who called you out of darkness into His wonderful light. Once you were not a people, *but now you are the people of God*; once you had not received mercy, but now you have received mercy (I Peter 2:9-10, emphasis added).

This is not to say that the Church has replaced the covenant God made with Israel, but that the promise of being "called" extends to His Church as part of the New Testament dispensation (cf. Jeremiah 31:31-32). After the parenthetical period (where Israel is temporarily in the background of

God's view) expires at the Rapture of the Church, the Lord will resume His direct dealings with Israel. Until that time, the Church is God's primary focus.

A noteworthy a parallel may be drawn to the Church with regard to Israel. Just as Israel was called to a higher standard than the surrounding nations, so too is the Church called to a higher calling than the unbelieving world in which it is placed. Because we too have been given the oracles of God in the New Testament that includes the plan of salvation in Christ, it is expected of us to live lives commensurate with those gifts. Simply stated, the promise and benefits of being *called out* by God comes at a price. This price is the expectation of setting an example to the world by holy living. This truth is well established in Scripture: "As obedient children, do not conform to the evil desires you had when you lived in ignorance. *But just as He who called you is holy, so be holy in all you do; for it is written: 'Be holy, because I am holy'*" (I Peter 1:14-15, emphasis added).

The general population, the unbelieving world, is *not expected* to live holy lives. Because the general population is ignorant of God's expectations as prescribed in Scripture, they are not being addressed in our theme.[6] God's people are those who believe in the God of Israel and His Word, the Bible. God's people are those who believe His promises of salvation, provision and protection. God's people are those who obey Him. God's people are those who defend His

---

[6] John MacArthur, *Can God Bless America?* (Nashville, TN: W Publishing Group, 2002), 6.

honor, who stand up against the forces determined to remove His rightful place in our nation; those who defend His name. Further, God's people are those who believe He will fight our battles when our nation, our church, our family, or our lives are threatened. This truth is made clear in God's Word in the account of David versus the Philistine giant, Goliath. David, who represented God's people Israel at a time of crisis explained this divine protection when he said: "All those gathered here will know that it is not by sword or spear that the Lord saves; *for the battle is the Lord's* and He will give all of you into our hands" (I Samuel 17:47, emphasis added).

David did not need armor or conventional weapons when confronting the giant since God had proven to him that He could easily save the nation apart from human instrumentality. So too is this truth relative to today's battle whether it be on a national or a home front.

More recently, the American patriot, Patrick Henry, who had a deep, unwavering trust in Divine Providence, asserted the same truth when he spoke at Richmond, Virginia, on March 23, 1775, before the War of Independence: ". . . we shall not fight our battles alone. There is a just God who presides over the destinies of nations; and He will raise up friends to fight our battles for us . . ."[7]

This kind of trust in the providence of God makes up the character of God's people, be it the covenant nation of Israel

---

[7] Peter A. Lillback, *Freedom's Holy Light*, (Bryn Mawr, PA: The Providence Forum, 2000), 10.

or His people, the Church.

Who Are Not God's People

To avoid confusion as to what God is saying to *His* people, we should distinguish who are *not* God's people. Any nation or people opposed to the God of the Israel, the God of the Bible, are *not* God's people. Moses spoke God's covenant regarding those who were alienated toward Him when he wrote: "Make sure there is no man or woman, clan or tribe among you today *whose heart turns away from the LORD our God to go and worship the gods of those nations*; make sure there is no root among you that produces such bitter poison" (Deuteronomy 29:18, emphasis added).

Who are not God's people of His Church today? Simply, those who do not have a personal relationship with Him through his Son, Jesus Christ, and accordingly, go and worship the (heathen) gods of other nations. Hearing this, one may say: "Americans do not worship the gods of heathen nations!" But is that really true? We are in fact worshipping the gods of humanism, materialism, hedonism, narcissism, sensualism, and egotism. This places us in the same category as heathen idolaters.

This lack of a personal relationship with Christ prevents us from seeing God's view of biblical values. God's people do not sanction homosexuality, approve of abortions, ascribe to child pornography on the Internet , or other vices that may be protected under the First Amendment. God's people have not bought into the value system Paul describes in Romans chapter one. Here is a partial list of our changing value system that is a modern view of Romans chapter one born out of those who are not God's people:

Changing Values
They exchanged the truth of God for a lie, and worshiped and served created things rather than the Creator-- who is forever praised. Romans 1:25 (NIV)

BIBLICAL TERM	MODERN TERM
SEXUAL SINS[8]	
Abortion	Pro-Choice
Fornication/ Perversion	Casual Sex; Voyeurism
Homosexuality	Gay/Alternate Lifestyle; Same-Sex Marriage
Pornography	Adult Movies; Exotic Art
Incest	Not Invented Yet
Bestiality	Not Invented Yet
Transvestism	Cross Dressing (Transgenderism)
Adultery	Flirtation; Wife-Swapping, Swinging

Social Sins[9]

---

[8] Ex. 20:13; I Cor. 6:13, 18; 7:2; Eph. 5:3; Ex. 22:19; Lev. 18:22-23; 20:13-16; Rom. 1:24-27; I Cor. 6:9-11; Hab. 1:13; Lev. 18:19; 20:12, 17; Deut. 27:22; Ex. 22:19; Lev. 18:23; 20:10; Deut. 22:5, 22; 27:21; Lev. 20:10.

[9] Gen. 2:24; Deut. 24:1-4; Mal. 2:15-16; I Cor. 7:17; Mt. 5:31-32; 19:8-9; Lk. 16:17-18; Ex. 20:4; Eph. 5:5; Col. 3:5; Lk. 16:19; Col. 2:8; Ex. 12:12-14; 22:18; Lev. 24:17, 21; Rom. 13:13; I Cor. 5:11; 6:10; Eph. 5:18; I Thess. 5:7-8; Prov. 13:11; Deut. 18:10-13; Prov. 6:4, 9-10; 10:4-5; 20:13; 23:21; 13:24; 22:15; Ex. 20:17; 2 Tim. 2:16; Eph. 4:29; Col. 3:8; Prov. 11:15;

Divorce	Irreconcilable Differences
Idolatry	Materialism
Idolatry	Humanism
Death Penalty	Cruelty
Drug Abuse	Legalized Drugs
Alcoholism	Social Drinking
Gambling	Stock Trading; Sports/Lottery Pools, etc.
Divination/Witchcraft	Astrology; Horoscope
Indolence	Welfare
Disciplining Children	Child Abuse
Covetousness	Ambition
Profanity	Freedom of Expression
Surety	Collateral
Indebtedness/Borrowing	Bankruptcy
Usury	Loans; Pawn-Brokering

The above table reads like the American daily newspaper, with society reaching the level of not tolerating any person or institution making moral judgments that would condemn the practices they enjoy. As long as this prevailing mindset continues, God cannot bless our nation.

God is looking to bless America if and when America makes the God of Israel, the God of the Bible, its God. The psalmist proclaimed that when God's people trusted Him as their God—their only god—blessings would follow: "Blessed is the nation whose God is the LORD, the people he chose for his inheritance" (Ps. 33:12).

17:18; 22:26; Ps. 37:21; Rom. 13:8; Deut. 22:19; 2 Tim. 3:16; 2 Pet. 1:21.

When Secretary of the Treasury Salmon P. Chase wrote to the director of the U. S. Mint in Philadelphia to introduce the motto, "In God We Trust" in November 20, 1861, he wrote the following explanation: "No nation can be strong except in the strength of God or safe except in His defense. The trust of our people in God should be declared on our national coins."[10]

Congress adopted Chase's proposal and President Lincoln signed the proposal into law shortly before he was assassinated. In 1956, "In God We Trust" was declared to be the official motto of the United States. "In these simple words, our government declared that America was itself unashamedly a faith-based institution in the ultimate sense of trusting in a God who rules over and protects His people."[11]

In June 2002, the 9th Circuit U. S. Court of Appeals declared that the words "under God" in the Pledge of Allegiance are unconstitutional. The author of the attack on the nation's Pledge triumphantly declared that he was going after the national motto, "In God We Trust," next.

If God's people allow these attacks on our national heritage to continue unchallenged and without a fight, we deserve God's wrath. George Washington warned the nation against the mindset that leads to disregarding eternal rules when he wrote:

---

[10] Peter A. Lillback, *Freedom's Holy Light*, (Bryn Mawr, PA: The Providence Forum, 2000), 19.

[11] Peter A. Lillback, *Freedom's Holy Light*, (Bryn Mawr, PA: The Providence Forum, 2000), 20.

> No people can be bound to acknowledge and adore the Invisible Hand which conducts the affairs of men more than the people of the United States . . . We ought to be no less persuaded that *the propitious smiles of Heaven can never be expected on a nation that disregards the eternal rules of order and right which Heaven itself has ordained* (emphasis added)[12]

In order for God to bless our nation, God's people must be the first to repent. If there is to be any revival for America, it must first begin in the House of God.

---

[12] Peter A. Lillback, *Freedom's Holy Light*, (Bryn Mawr, PA: The Providence Forum, 2000), 15.

Dr. Ralph D. Curtin

2
Who are The "Called" By God's Name?

Do we still hold to the right of calling ourselves a Christian nation? By comparing Alex DeToqueville's early depiction of our country in 1831 with today's picture, it gives rise to the answer that we can no longer call ourselves by that title: "Not until I went into the churches of American and heard her pulpits flame with righteousness did I understand the secret of her genius and power. America is great because America is good, and if America ever ceases to be good, America will cease to be great."[13]

With the changing values chart exhibited in the previous chapter acting as a barometer on America today, it is obvious that our pulpits and our legislators are not living up to the standards observed by DeToqueville. We can hardly call ourselves a "Christian nation."

On the reverse side of the dollar bill, opposite the great seal of America, is the pyramid that speaks of the Providence of God. Above the unfinished pyramid is a great eye in a triangle surrounded by radiance. "The eye of Providence in a triangle is a symbol depicting God the Father."[14] Above the eye are the words *Annuit Coeptis*, the Latin motto for "He has smiled on our undertakings," a phrase taken from Virgil by Charles Thompson, Secretary to the Continental Congress. The phrase conveys the faith of America at that

---

[13] Peter A. Lillback, *Freedom's Holy Light*, (Bryn Mawr, PA: The Providence Forum , 2000), 1.
[14] Ibid, 6.

time, believing that God's providence had blessed America's founders and their purpose to establish a Christian nation.

In the shadow of subversive groups working overtime to rid our nation of prayer (in schools, in the Supreme Court, etc.) it is inspiring to note that the first official act of the First Continental Congress back in 1774 was to open in prayer.

Based on the comparison of then to now, we are forced to recognize that our nation is no longer the "Christian nation" it once was and therefore, we as a nation are not the "called" by God's name. No, not even the "religious" can claim to be *called* by God's name.

The "Religious" Are Not Called by God's Name

The French philosopher, Blaise Pascal, in 1623 wrote, "Men never do evil so completely and cheerfully as when they do it from religious conviction." In modern times, Charles Colson applied Pascal's principle to our culture where he wrote: "Outwardly, we are a religious people, but inwardly our religious beliefs make no difference in how we live. We are obsessed with self; we live, raise families, govern, and die as though God does not exist, just as Nietzsche predicted a century ago. God is tolerated in the media only when He is bland enough to pose no threat."[15]

Remembering that it was the religious people of Jesus' day (the Sanhedrin, the Pharisees, the Sadducees) that

---

[15] Charles W. Colson, *Kingdoms In Conflict*, (Grand Rapids, MI: Zondervan Publishing House, 1987), 214.

condemned Him and handed Him over to the Roman authorities to be executed helps us to keep both Pascal and Colson's observations in their correct perspective. It is *not* the *religious* who are called by God's name.

The "Called" By God's Name

In Deuteronomy chapter seven, the Lord adds to the definition of the "called" we established in Chapter One. He said: "The Lord did not set his affections on you [covenant Israel] and choose you because you were more numerous than other peoples, for you were the fewest of all peoples. But it was *because the Lord loved you and kept the oath he swore to your forefathers* that he brought you out with a mighty hand and redeemed you from the land of slavery..." (Deuteronomy 7:7-8, emphasis added).

Clearly God's "called" is covenant Israel, chosen out of God's love for them. While it's true that God's love extends to His entire creation [that's why He sent His Son to die on the Cross (cf. John 3:16)], His gift of salvation does not. This is because Christ's death rendered the world "savable," but not all men will be saved, and therefore not all are "called."[16] The "called," in the New Testament are the "elect," drawn from the entire pool of humanity in the world regardless of

---

[16] The issue of the "elect" and "called" of God is addressed in *Things Which Become Sound Doctrine*, by Dwight Pentecost (Grand Rapids, MI: Kregal Puplications, 1996), under the topic Reconciliation. Here Pentecost explains that "God, in Christ Jesus, was changing the relationship of the world to Himself so that men in the world are now savable" (86, emphasis added).

their nationality or religious background.

Jesus clearly distinguished the *elect* from the world in his great intercessory prayer where He said, "I pray for them [the *elect*]. *I am not praying for the world*, but for those you have given me, for they are yours" (John 17:9, emphasis added).

Further, Christ specifically labels His believers the "elect" in the great eschatological discourse in Matthew 24: "If those days had not been cut short, no one would survive, but for the sake of the *elect* those days will be shortened ... and he will send his angels with a loud trumpet call, and they will gather his *elect* from the four winds, from one of the heavens to the other (vv. 22, 31, emphasis added).

Paul reiterates Christ's position on the world vs. the *called* or *elect*. The "called" are also those *elect* in the church, being chosen by the members of the Triune Godhead before time began: "For he chose us in him before the creation of the world to be holy and blameless in his sight. In love he predestined us to be adopted as his sons through Jesus Christ, in accordance with his pleasure and will" (Ephesians 1:4-5).

Again, in the great doctrinal book of Romans, Paul affirms the separation of the *elect* from the world: "Who shall lay anything to the charge of God's *elect*? It is God that justifieth" (Romans 8:33 KJV, emphasis added) [note: *elect* is rendered "chosen" in the NIV].

Peter, too, separates out the chosen in the Church from the world. He also calls them the *elect*: "Peter, an apostle of Jesus Christ, to God's *elect*, strangers in the world . . . who have been *chosen* according to the foreknowledge of God the

Father through the sanctifying work of the Spirit . . ." (I Peter 1:1-2, emphasis added).

It is a settled issue in Scripture as to who are the "called" by God's Name, they are the *elect*, those who have been saved by the blood of Christ and regenerated by the Holy Spirit.[17] They are not the unconverted public of the world.

The Elect Must Stand Up and Be Counted

"When the wicked repent, God will bless America!" This statement is not biblical and the root to a common error pervading our modern church. This common error in Bible teaching today can be traced back to the account of God's destruction on the cities of Sodom and Gomorrah located in Genesis 18-19. Here is the account of what happens when the righteous *do not* stand up and be counted:

> X The angel of the Lord (the pre-incarnate Christ, cf. John 8:56, 58) appears to Abraham and explains to him that the wicked behavior of the Sodomites in committing homosexuality can no longer be tolerated, and that destruction has been

---

[17] The work of Regeneration is especially ascribed in the Scriptures to the Holy Spirit (cf. John 3:5-8; Titus 3:5). It is the spiritual change wrought in man by the operation of the Holy Spirit, by which he becomes the possessor of a new life. Regeneration must include the transformation of the spiritual and moral nature as evidence of salvation.

decreed.

X Abraham intercedes on behalf of the righteous and begins a bargaining process with the Angel of the Lord, beginning with fifty and finally agreeing on ten. If there are ten righteous, God will spare the city (cf. 18:24, 32).

X When two angels appear at Lot's home (Abraham's nephew), who is living in the city of Sodom, they are accosted by the homosexuals, bringing the angels to smite them with blindness. The angels then declare that they cannot destroy the city unless the righteous are first removed (19:12-13, 16, 22).

X Once Lot and his family (total of four) were safely out of the city, the Angel of the Lord called down fire and brimstone from the Lord in heaven, destroying the city and all the inhabitants (19:24).

The key to this terrible act of judgment is found in the truth that destruction came upon the city not because of the gross wickedness being committed by the unbelievers, *but because of the lack of righteous people* standing up for what was right. If there were but ten righteous, the city would have been spared. This narrative clearly admonishes the *elect*, (the believer; the righteous) that they must stand up and be counted. A similar fate came to the antediluvian civilization in the time of Noah. Of the five billion persons alive at that time, only eight stood up and were saved

(Genesis 7:13).[18]

The tendency for the *elect* or God's *chosen* to sit on the sidelines and allow wickedness to overtake them is not new. The same condition was evident in Jerusalem just prior to the Babylonian invasion when Israel was taken captive for seventy years. After Jehovah listed Israel's sins, claiming they could not distinguish between the holy and the profane, He declared through Ezekiel: "I looked for a man among them who would build up the wall and stand before me in the gap on behalf of the land so I would not have to destroy it, but I found none" (Ezekiel 22:30).

> Lenin particularly hated seriously committed Christians. Weak Christians he could manage, but serious Christians meant nothing but trouble for a Marxist-Leninist regime. --- Charles W. Colson, *Kingdoms in Conflict*, 205.

Today, the eyes of the Lord range throughout the earth to strengthen those whose hearts are fully committed to Him, those who are willing to stand in the gap between the pull of the world and the desire to serve the Lord as a serious Christian. Perhaps the "elect" need to be humbled in order for God to raise up those who will stand in the gap.

---

[18] The figure of five billion persons being alive at the time of the Flood is arrived at through a population model discussed in the book, *Scientific Creationism*, by Henry M. Morris (Green Forest, AR: Master Books, 1996).

3
Humbling Ourselves

In Isaiah chapter nine, prior to the fall of the Northern Kingdom of Israel in 722 B.C., God warned the Southern Kingdom of Judah that she too would be destroyed if she persisted in the activities that characterized the North. But Israel's leadership believed that they would experience only a mild setback and in turn they would easily rebuild their nation, if not even stronger than before the enemy invaded. Because of their arrogance, the prophet lamented that even though Israel would suffer at the hand of God through the Assyrians, they still would not return to Him. In turn, their continued refusals and denials of their sins would lead to more judgment. Accordingly, Israel would suffer judgment in several forms: from God, their enemies the Assyrians, and internal corruption and wickedness. It seems that after this national disaster would strike Israel, they would revert to pride rather than humble themselves before their God.

Unfortunately, America is following the path Israel took during this period.

After the attacks on our nation on September 11, 2001, America responded with pride in its military and economic might. Religions, too, seemed to galvanize when religious leaders from many different faiths petitioned God's favor to protect our nation from further harm and to invoke His healing powers on our land. These honorable steps bolstered the nation's pride and intestinal fortitude—and even promoted unity—but did nothing to move our nation toward humility. God is looking for this character trait in order to bless our nation.

God, in turn, has dramatically allowed the world's support system to fail in order to demonstrate that in our pride, we cannot look to them for protection. As powerful as our military and law enforcement agencies are, they are finding it increasingly difficult to ferret out all the terrorists from their dirty holes. From international terrorists in Afghanistan to sniper terrorists in Virginia, it sounds like God is saying, "You cannot put all your confidence in the military or in law enforcement." When a church undergoes ethical and moral failure in scandals surrounding sexual abuses, God is clearing saying, "You cannot put your confidence in religion." When the Enron, WorldCom, Global Crossing, Tyco and ImClone scandals seriously undermined the nation's confidence in corporate finance, God is clearly saying, "You cannot put your confidence in monetary resources." These failures point to the truth that our confidence as a nation, a church, a family, and as individuals cannot be independent of God, but most assuredly must be *in* God. Jeremiah attempted to warn the nation of Judah that judgment was inevitable if they did not turn from putting their confidence in their resources or evil alliances: "This is what the Lord says: Cursed is the one who trusts in man, who depends on flesh for his strength and whose heart turns away from the Lord. Blessed is the man [or nation] who trusts in the Lord, whose *confidence* is in him" (Jeremiah 17:5, 7, emphasis added).

Judah, like America, did not learn from experience. The adage reads: If there is anything that we have learned from experience, it is that we have learned *nothing* by experience.

George Santayana in *Life of Reason* put it this way: "Those who fail to learn from the past are condemned to repeat it." Unless America, the Church, or the individual recognizes their failures, they are doomed to repeat them.

Humbleness Is the Answer

James tells the Christian that "God opposes the proud, but gives grace to the humble" (4:6). Later he adds, "Humble yourselves before the Lord and He will lift you up" (4:11). His description of being humble (Gr. *tapeinoo*) is defined as a condition of the heart that embraces the act of being humiliated, cast down, or submissive. This is the opposite of a prideful heart that is arrogant, egotistical, or presumptuous.

After the September 11, 2001, attacks on our nation, America did not respond in a godly fashion. Neither did the Body of Christ respond in a godly fashion. Nor did the individual on the street respond in a godly fashion. While the nation was entitled to retaliate and seek revenge as a result of that act of war, the nation missed out on the blessing of receiving God's grace by not humbling themselves before Him. As a nation and as a Church, had we sought the Lord for cause and repented of our sin, He would have forgiven our sin and healed our land. However, the record shows that the nation's Christian churches had no significant change after 9/11. If there were no changes in the Church, can we expect change from the non-Christian man on the street? A change that emerges out of being humiliated, cast down, and even to a degree, submissive to the hand of God that allowed this to happen? No, not yet. This is the reason why the Christian church is so anxious today, because they have not found rest or peace for their souls. The rest that emerges out of humbleness is a God-thing: "Take my yoke upon you and learn from me, for I am gentle and *humble* in heart, and you will find *rest* for your souls" (Matthew 11:29, emphasis added).

The Christ-like quality of humbleness comes from the proper relationship with Christ where the Christian takes on His yoke (the heart of a lowly, humble servant), seeking to perform the will of God in their lives. It is not a self-seeking, self-satisfying life, but one of self-sacrifice in order to find the rest promised. And with this rest comes peace.

Humbleness Leads To the Peace of God

The world is feverishly searching for peace. Not a detente that is simply the lessening of hostility offered by the world, but the kind of lasting peace that only comes from God. It is a curious thing in the Bible how God contrasts two different kinds of peace: peace with God and the peace of God.

> X Peace With God. This peace is the work of Christ into which the individual enters by faith upon salvation. We are then justified, bringing peace with God. The issue of hostility between the sinner and his Creator has been settled (Rom. 5:1; Eph. 2:14-17).
> X Peace Of God. This peace is quite different from Peace With God. Many Christians fail to enjoy

this special peace since it is only granted to those entering into the interior life with Christ. This inward peace, the state of the soul and spirit of the Christian who, having entered into peace with God, has now committed all their anxieties to God through prayer and a trusting relationship (Jn. 14:27; Phil. 4:7; Col. 3:15).

Once the Christians have humbled themselves before God and admitted that they have sought refuge and support elsewhere–only to have it end in folly–then they are on the path to restoration. This humbleness can lead to the wonderful interior life that offers what many Christians have experienced, the peace of God.

Dr. Ralph D. Curtin

4
Why We Should Pray

There are many reasons why the Christian should pray, but the most important is, God tells us to do so. Prayer then becomes an act of obedience.

> Look to the Lord and his strength; seek his face always (1 Chronicles 16:11). And pray in the Spirit on all occasions with all kinds of prayers and requests (Ephesians 6:18).

If God commands us to pray in both testaments, He must have a good reason. When we obey God by praying, He opens up the pathways to His dwelling place as it is a sweet-smelling aroma to Him; obedience being preferred to any sacrificial offering (I Samuel 15:22). This act of obedience leads to worship where the Christian communes with his Creator to maintain fellowship. This is a crucial reason to pray.

Earnest prayer also leads to examination of the heart before the Lord. This step enables us to agree with God over any sin that may be obstructing our relationship with Him, bringing us to the place where we confess and repent of it. "Examine yourselves to see whether you are in the faith; test yourselves. Do you not realize that Christ Jesus is in you—unless, of course, you fail the test" (II Corinthians 13:5).

Any guilt or frustrations that emerge from sinful behavior should be dealt with in prayer. God grants us a release through prayer. Any spiritual, emotional or physical emergencies that emerge from life should also be dealt with in prayer. Why? Because God grants us a release in prayer. Once we are *clean* before God, we have the confidence that He hears us (I John 3:21).

Prayer Is Vital For Change

In addition to opening a channel to God that leads to self-examination, prayer brings change. Andrew Murray notes: "Beware in your prayer, above everything, of limiting God, not only by unbelief, but by fancying that you know what he can do."[18] God, the author of change, can be expected to change either the circumstances, the outcome, or the heart of the petitioner to accept whatever the answer from the Lord is: Yes, No, or Not Now.

Prayer changes things. This adage carries a tremendous message. When a nation, a church, or an individual Christian has moved away from God, often bringing undesirable consequences, prayer can initiate the process of change that ends in restoration. An example of this is seen in the life of Hezekiah, the twelfth king of Judah (715-686 B.C.). When the Assyrian king, Sennacherib, threatened Hezekiah's kingdom with annihilation, Hezekiah was driven to his knees in prayer, crying out to the Lord for deliverance from his enemy. Shortly afterward, Isaiah the prophet sent a message to Hezekiah saying: "This is what the Lord, the God of Israel, says, 'I have heard your prayer concerning Sennacherib king of Assyria ... He [Sennacherib] shall not

---

[18] Edythe Draper, *Draper's Book of Quotations for the Christian World* (Wheaton, IL: Tyndale House Publishers, Inc., 1992). Entries 8757-8759.

enter the city or shoot an arrow here. I will defend this city and save it, for my sake and for the sake of David my servant'" (II Kings 19:20, 32, 34).

God miraculously changed the circumstances where we read: "That night the angel of the Lord went out and put to death a hundred and eighty-five thousand men in the Assyrian camp. When the people got up the next morning—there were all the dead bodies! So Sennacherib king of Assyrian broke camp and withdrew. He returned to Nineveh and stayed there" (II Kings 19:35-36).

This is the kind of change we can expect—miraculous—when we pray to God! Abraham Lincoln believed in prayer and said, "I have been driven many times to my knees by the overwhelming conviction that I had nowhere else to go. My own wisdom and that of those about me seemed insufficient for the day."[19]

God is still in the miracle business! He is still in the *changing* business as well. If God can protect Israel from an invading enemy when the king or national leader and his people prayed, thereby changing the course of events, can He not perform that miracle for America when we become a praying nation?

When the Christian prays, other great things happen as well. Concerted prayer can lead to revival, nationally and

> "All the Christian virtues are locked up in the word ***prayer***."
> --Charles Spurgeon, (*Draper's Book of Quotations*)

[19] Edythe Draper, *Draper's Book of Quotations for the Christian World* (Wheaton, IL: Tyndale House Publishers, Inc., 1992). Entries 8757-8759.

individually. In Christ's parable of the persistent widow (Luke 18:1-7), He gives instructions that encourage men to pray always and never give up. This constant solicitude to God for our nation, our church, and our family will not go unheeded by God. This parable clearly states that God will answer prayers, especially those for justice against our adversaries.

Prayer to Avoid Further Calamities

The final reason the Christian should pray is to avoid further calamities. John MacArthur notes:

> "Sadly, when sin is not confronted, sinners do not perceive their need for grace and forgiveness. Frankly, our nation is in no position at the moment to be blessed. *We're actually more likely to be cursed by God"*[19] (emphasis added).

MacArthur also explains how America has no guarantee that God will continue to bless our nation. Come to think about it, the "insurance" protection we have received from God based on the faith and biblical convictions of our founding fathers who drafted up the documents we live by today, has long since expired, and we are living in the *grace period* with the policy about to expire!

---

[19] John Macarthur, *Can God Bless America?*, (Nashville, TN: W Publishing Gr,) 8.

Yet, it is not too late for our nation to repent and expect God to bless us. We call to mind the harrowing account of the impending destruction of the wicked city of Nineveh and how God used the reluctant prophet, Jonah, to get the message of God to those recalcitrant people before it was too late. Once they heard Jonah's cry of judgment, they embraced God's gift of repentance. He then extended His forgiveness and healed their land.

This is what can happen here in America.

5
Why Seek After God's Face?

There has been a great departure away from God in America. Americans are following after pagan nations by deliberately, and in many cases, unwittingly, seeking after false gods. The God of the Bible will not tolerate this sin of idolatry. He must honor His first commandment, "You shall have no other gods before me" (Exodus 20:3). This command was further delineated so that the children of Israel would be clear as to what God meant. "Do not make idols or set up an image or a sacred stone for yourselves, and do not place a carved stone in your land to bow down before it. I am the Lord your God" (Leviticus 26:1). Signs of America's wayward hearts can be documented in a recent Barna Research Survey that maintains that a "large share of the people who attend Protestant or Catholic churches have adopted beliefs that conflict with the teachings of the Bible and their church." He elaborates on those conflicts:

- Six out of ten Americans (59%) reject the existence of Satan, indicating that the devil, or Satan, is merely a symbol of evil.
- What is surprising is the large share of Protestants that believe in praying to dead saints, a notion dismissed by most Protestant churches. Amazingly, one out of six evangelicals (16%) and half of the non-evangelical born again Christians (50%) also believe in praying to dead saints. More than one-third of the public (35%) also believes that it is

"possible to communicate with others after they die." Three out of ten non-evangelical born again Christians believe in communication with the dead.

- Although most adults are aligned with either a Protestant (54%) or Catholic (22%) church, a large minority of Americans believe that when Jesus Christ was on earth He committed sins.

- Protection from eternal condemnation for one's sins is widely considered to be earned rather than received as a free gift from God. Half of all adults (50%) argue that anyone who "is generally good or does enough good things for others during their life will earn a place in Heaven." Apparently, large numbers of the non-evangelical born again adults believe that people have a choice of means to salvation, either the grace-alone or the salvation-through-works approaches.

- The concept of original sin (imputation) is rejected by most Americans in favor of a rational choice to human nature.

- Regarding sources of truth: This is perhaps most clearly evident through the finding that a plurality of adults (44%) contends that, "the Bible, the Koran and the Book of Mormon are all different expressions of the same spiritual truths."

These statistics show a rising tendency on the part of Americans to abandon the fundamentals of this nation's Christian founders. These departures indicate that there is an increasing element of Americans that are confused as to sources of faith and truth, and accordingly, turning away from seeking after the face of the God of the Bible.

Some examples of our nation seeking after other gods may not be found in sacred stones, but are clearly evident in other forms:

> 1. Americans now embrace gods that are not of the Bible. American college students have been required to read a book about the Quran. This religious coercion included chanting and the call to prayer.[20] One could only imagine the public outcry from students if they were required to read John 3:16 and pray to receive Christ as Savior?
>
> 2. The god Adar'melech, a form of the Syrian god Hadad. This deity was worshipped in NW Mesopotamia by the burning of children (II Kings 17:31). Today this god is honored in America through abortions as a way of life; a way of birth control. An example of our honoring this god was recently seen in Florida. Before losing a lawsuit brought against them, the Broward County, School Board, actually taught children not only where they can get an abortion, but how they could get an abortion, how much abortions cost and how they could keep their parents from finding out they were getting an abortion.[21]

---

[20] "College Sued Over Quran Book Reading," *American Family Association Newsletter*, September, 2002.

[21] Paul Hoffman, *The Salt And Light Solution.* (Fort Lauderdale, FL: Coral Ridge Ministries, 1999), 53.

3. The god Anath is the Canaanite patroness of sex, the paramour of Aliyan Baal. America's infatuation with sex has become cultish.

4. Ar'temis, the Greek goddess, also known among the Romans as Diana is the patron god of nature and wild animals. Today, the Redwoods, the manatee, the sea turtle, and the snail darter are protected under federal law while the unborn human can be killed in the womb by the abortionist's surgical tool.

5. Ashe'rah, a pagan goddess found in N. Syria and Tyre in the fifteenth century B. C., had as her cult object a phallic symbol depicted in stone pillars representing the male organ to honor the male god Baal. These gods promoted homosexuality ("male prostitutes" and "sodomites") (Deut. 23:18, marg.; I Ki. 14:24; 15:12; 22:46). This god also glamorized lust and murder in the Canaanite religion. The Syrian deity Rimmon was worshipped for the same reasons. Both homosexuality and murder is glamorized in our society today.

6. Gad, rendered "fortune" (Isaiah 65:11, marg). A Canaanite deity that stood for "good luck." Americans "consult" this god when seeking a quick fortune through astrology or other mediums on how and when they should make investments or gamble on lottery tickets, sporting events, etc.

7. Hermes, the Greek god who served as protector of commerce and trade. The favor of this impotent god is unwittingly called upon when seeking to

buy or sell something of value.

8. Ba'al-ze'bub. The form of the name of Baal worshiped by the Philistines. It is a matter of divine revelation that demonism is the dynamic of idolatry (I Corinthians 10:20). Behind the heathen deities were evil spirits or demons. Today, modern America is enamored with demonic activity as found in fiction (movies, books, etc.) and children's toys (Ouija board; Pok'e-mon; Yu-Ge-Oh, etc.).

9. The Shaggy Goat. This reference is to demonic creatures that would dance among the ruins of Babylon to some object of idolatrous reverence (Lev. 17:7; Isa. 13:21). This corresponds with any material object that is worshipped before the Lord. In our materialist society, the parallel is easily drawn where we read on the bumper sticker, "He who dies with the most toys, wins."[22]

The admonition given to Moses and Joshua prior to entering into the promised land regarding Israel's propensity to descend into idolatry went unheeded, so the Lord turned His face away from them and brought disaster on them. Jehovah warned:

> And the Lord said to Moses: "You are going to rest with your fathers, and these people will soon prostitute themselves to the foreign gods of the land they are entering. They will forsake me and break the covenant I made with them. On that day I will become angry with them and forsake them; I will hide

my face from them, and they will be destroyed. Many disasters and difficulties will come upon them, and on that day they will ask, 'Have not these disasters come upon us because our God is not with us?' And I will certainly hide my face on that day because of all their wickedness in turning to other gods" (Deuteronomy 31:16-18).

America too, when left to its own devices has fallen into idolatry, allowing man's depraved nature to dominate him and control his form of worship. Without God intervening, we would stay in that state. This is why we must seek after God's face if we, as a nation, are to be blessed.

---

[22]*The New Unger's Bible Dictionary.* (Chicago, IL: Moody Press, Biblesoft Program, 1988).

Seeking after God's Face Brings Blessings

Seeking after the God of the Bible to make Him the God of our nation will bring blessings upon our land. But just as the Lord permits an individual to harden their heart against Him, as He did in the case of the Pharaoh of the Exodus, so too does He permit a nation to harden their hearts against Him. Of course this has been demonstrated over the eons by Israel hardening their heart to the voice of the prophets. God, then, had no alternative but to bring chastisement upon them. God in His graciousness often opens a "spiritual window" to permit man to respond to His call before chastisement is brought upon them. I believe God opened a "spiritual window," on September 11, 2001—an opportunity for our nation to respond to God's call—to turn back to Him, to seek His face. This is how He expressed this "open window" concept to his beloved Israel: "Seek the Lord while he may be found; call on him while he is near. Let the wicked forsake his way and the evil man his thoughts. Let him turn to the Lord and he will have mercy on him, and to our God, for he will freely pardon" (Isaiah 55:6-7).

This seeking after the Lord's face while He may be found in many cases leads to salvation, the greatest blessing God can bestow on a nation or individual. John MacArthur adds: "The greatest blessings God has graciously given America have been *spiritual* blessings—knowledge of the good news of salvation in Christ, freedom for the gospel to be propagated, sweeping revivals like those of the Great Awakenings, and growth and spiritual prosperity for the church in our nation."²³

Progressive revelation, together with systematic theology, demonstrates that Moses, while not permitted to look upon the face of God, did indeed, as the result of his search, see the face of God. This appearance of the face of God was the pre-incarnate manifestation of Christ (cf. Ex. 24:9-10; 33:20; Jn. 5:37; 10:30; 14:6-9), testifying to the truth that searching

---

²³John MacArthur, *Can God Bless America?* (Nashville, TN: W Publishing Group, 2002), vii.

after God's face will bring Him closer to you: "Then you will call upon me and come and pray to me, and I will listen to you. You will seek me and find me when you seek me with all your heart. I will be found by you, declares the Lord. . ." (Jeremiah 29:12-14).

Paradoxically, in our humanity, we seek after God when we are in a state of crisis. Historically, as a nation, a church, and as individuals, we turn to the Lord out of necessity or affliction. This was a cyclical practice with Israel, and we in America must learn from *their* mistakes and not to make our own by waiting until another disaster comes upon us before we seek God's face: "And they will seek my face; in their misery they will earnestly seek me" (Hosea 5:15).

CHAPTER 6
Turning From Our Wicked Ways

Are we a Christian nation? At one time America could unequivocally say, *"Yes."* Our nation's patriarchs affirmed this in the very documents that undergird our democracy. "The Declaration of Independence specifically refers to God four times, the last appeals to 'the protection of Divine Providence.'" Thomas Jefferson, one of our nation's leading patriarchs, knew that providence meant the intervention of God in the affairs of men throughout history. Trusting in "Providence" as a nation means that we believe God is the power sustaining and guiding human destiny. Jefferson's Address of 1801 uses language consistent with his trust in Providence:

> Let us, then, with courage and confidence pursue our own federal and republican principles ... enlight-

ened by a benign religion, professed, indeed, and practiced in various forms, yet all of them including honesty, truth, temperance, gratitude, and the love of man; acknowledging and *adoring an overruling Providence which by all its dispensations* proves that it delights in the happiness of man here and his greater happiness hereafter (emphasis added).[24]

This language is further used extensively in his Second Address of 1805: ". . . of that Being in whose hands we are . . . who has covered our infancy with His providence and our riper years with His wisdom and power . . ."

- We applaud Jefferson, yet sadly, we observe that our nation as a whole has turned away from God over the years. This fact is evident in America's treatment of vital biblical doctrine that helped form the foundation of our nation's government. The departure from biblical doctrine has a profound effect on the nation's view toward moral and ethical responses to life. The following transcript attests to this departure by a representative of America's clergy:"I believe Jesus the Messiah, the Christ of God was fully human. *The myth of the virgin birth* is found neither in Mark (the earliest gospel account) nor in John (the latest). A theological myth as you

---

[24] Peter A. Lillback, *Freedom's Holy Light.* (Bryn Mawr, PA: The Providence Forum, 2000), 3.

know so well is not false presentation, but a valid and quite persuasive literary device employed to point to ultimate truth that can only be insinuated symbolically and never depicted exhaustively.

•"*The myth of the virgin birth* was not intended as historical fact but was employed by Matthew and Luke in different ways to appoint poetically the truth about Jesus as experienced in the emerging church."

•"*Jesus was not born Christ*, rather by the confluence of grace with faith he became the Christ, God's beloved in who God was well pleased."

•"I believe in the resurrection of Jesus, *but I cannot believe that his resurrection involved the resuscitation of his physical body*."

•"I am certain that the miracle of the resurrection, preeminently that of Jesus, is *not tied to bodily resuscitation*. The linking of resurrection with bodily resuscitation is to make a literal religious proposition of a metaphorical symbolic expression of truth itself. This is the kind of idolatry from which I dissent."

•"*I must dissent from Christocentric exclusives which hold that Jesus is the only way to God's salvation*. Such an arrogant claim stands over and against the inclusive Jesus of the synoptics and limits God in ways that humans cannot and must not."

•"Our personal and communal lives will give credence or lack thereof to our witness and call others to, or repel them from the Jesus way, which I believe is unique and normative, *but not the only way to salvation.*"

• "In conclusion, simply stated, Jesus was fully human and fully divine. His humanity was given in his conception and birth *through the natural processes of procreation.* His divinity was derived, given as a gift, from his relationship of trust and obedience with God."[25]

If this degree of apostasy is found in America's church leadership, what can we expect from the man in the pew? This is a major cause of God's displeasure with America. The church leadership—not the secular world's leadership—is teaching heresy. The apostle Paul warned against such teachings in the final days and their acceptance by leading clergy signals America's turning away from God. He warns:

The Spirit clearly says that in

---

[25] Jim Cymbala, *Fresh Wind, Fresh Fire*. (Grand Rapids, MI: Zondervan Publishing House, 1997), 90.

>later times some will *abandon the faith* and follow deceiving spirits and things taught by demons. For the time will come when men will not put up with sound doctrine. Instead, to suit their own desires, they will gather around them a great number of teachers to say what their itching ears want to hear. They will turn their ears away from the truth and turn aside to *myths* (I Tim. 4:1; 2 Tim 4:3-4, emphasis added).

This apostasy is not restricted to any one church for as Jim Cymbala writes, it is widespread: "Christian researcher George Barna reports that 64% of 'born again' Americans and 40% of 'evangelical' Americans say there is no such thing as absolute truth. In other words, the Ten Commandments may or may not be valid, Jesus Christ isn't necessarily the only way to God and so forth."

This apostasy is rapidly encroaching in the church where a great number of seekers and members are not satisfied with biblical truth, nor spiritual fulfillment, but rather concentrate on social programs to meet their personal needs or flit from church to church in search of happiness based on natural desires. Spiritual obligation to serve the Lord is conspicuously absent in the church today.

This inordinate desire for Christians to integrate secular enterprises into their faith can be demonstrated by simply looking at the new tolerance manifested in their lifestyles. Instead of Christians being a godly influence on the non-Christian, the non-Christian has sway over the influence of the Christian. We can look at those Christian churches that integrate secular evolutionary teaching into Creationism. We can look at those Christian churches that argue for the perverted "prosperity gospel" that teaches the heretical doctrine that a wealthy Christian has received the fullness of Christ. We can look at those Christian churches that teach homosexuality as an alternative lifestyle while it is condemned in both Testaments. We can look at contemporary Christian music that often cannot be distinguished from secular music. We can look at those Christian churches that preach a "social" or "innocuous" gospel so as not to offend the person in the pew with the denunciation of sin. We can look at those Christian churches that teach moralism, espousing the lie that if America becomes moral God will bless our nation—as long as we hang up posters and flags that mention Him or return the Ten Commandments to the courtroom. MacArthur rightly observes, "But restoring Christian symbols to public places would be only cosmetic, like makeup on a harlot."[26]

Obviously, moralism is not the answer for as John MacArthur adds, "Remember this: It is people who consider themselves highly moral and deeply religious who are trying to kill Americans by flying airplanes into our buildings."[27] No, the Christian church cannot expect a change in our nation's values until there is a change of heart toward God. As Cymbala also comments,

---

[26] John MacArthur, *Can God Bless America?* (Nashville, TN: W Publishing Group, 2002), 75.

[27] John MacArthur, *Can God Bless America?* (Nashville, TN: W Publishing Group, 2002).

"The influence of filth and violence inpeople's lives will not be destroyed by polite talk" (or moralist thinking).[28] Action must be taken because Christians are tolerating sin by attempting moral reform while the real battle is spiritual reform. Yes, the Christian church needs spiritual reform where lives, not laws or dogma is changed. Only when the Christian, and the Church is *regenerated* (cf. Titus 3:5) according to the biblical mandate will there be any reform in America.[29]

Failure from Taking of the "Devoted Things"

Historically, Israel was not able to stand against its enemies when they took of the "devoted things" of the surrounding nations, those things that were designated by God for destruction. Presently, we in America cannot expect to stand against our enemies if we continue to take of the "devoted things" of the world that are designated by God for destruction.

In the Old Testament account of the conquest of Canaan in Joshua chapter 7, Joshua was instructed by God after the victory at Jericho to attack and conquer a Canaanite city located one-and-a-half miles from Bethel by the name of Ai. His military experts advised him to send only 2-3,000 men

[28] John MacArthur, *Can God Bless America?* (Nashville, TN: W Publishing Group, 2002) 96.

[29] Jim Cymbala, *Fresh Power*. (Grand Rapids, MI: Zondervan Publishing House, 2001), 38.

to complete the mission, citing that Ai was merely a city with a small military outpost. But the Israelites were routed by the enemy who gave chase and finally killed thirty-six of the Israelites.

Joshua went before the Lord in humiliation and was told that someone had taken of the "devoted things,"[30] from Jericho and that is why they cannot stand against their enemies. Joshua reflected on God's command to destroy with the sword everything that breathed (cf. Deut. 7:1-6; 20:16-18) and not to take any booty from the city unless told to do so and quickly recognized that there had been a violation. After a selection was determined that Achan had committed the crime and in turn he was brought before Joshua to face trial. Achan's confession reveals a four-step process that brought him to commit the deed:

- He saw the plunder. The lust of the eyes led to the commission of the act.
- He coveted. He quickly determined that what he saw, he wanted, regardless of the consequences.

---

[30] The work of Regeneration is especially ascribed in the Scriptures to the Holy Spirit (cf. Jn. 3:5-8; Titus 3:5). It is the spiritual change wrought in man by the operation of the Holy Spirit, by which he becomes the possessor of a new life. Regeneration must include the transformation of the spiritual and moral nature as evidence of salvation.

- He took. Natural impulses went unchecked and he reacted instinctively.

- He hid. Once the deed was done, the threat of discovery dictated concealment.

Achan's penalty was death. But his crime did not only impact on his life only, but on the life of his nation (displeasure from God; humiliation before their enemies; losing the battle), but also on his family. God commanded that his family be executed as well. This is a strong illustration that personal sin has a profound effect on our nation and our families.

In a very real way, the Christian church is like Achan. We are enraptured by the glitter of the world that we see. The carnal side of us is having sway where we want to be like the unbeliever, yet to be a Christian with all the spiritual rewards that go with it. In effect, we are coveting the "booty" of the world, and in many cases to the abandonment of our value system—often ignoring the consequences—all for the sake of temporary pleasures. Once we have ignored the prompting of the Holy Spirit warning us not to go any further, we fall into sin. We then take. After the deed, we attempt to conceal our act from others for fear of exposure.

It has been my experience that two factors contribute to divine judgment of a nation. (1) The nation's treatment of God's covenant people, Israel. (2) The nation's moral standards. Historically, any nation that supported Israel was blessed, while any nation that mistreated Israel was cursed.[31] As long as America

31"Devoted Things." The Hebrew term refers to the irrevocable giving over of things or persons to the Lord, often by totally destroying them.

> I have sinned against the Lord, the God of Israel. This is what I have done: When *I saw* in the plunder a beautiful robe from Babylonia, two hundred shekels of silver and a wedge of gold weighing fifty shekels, *I coveted* them and *took them.* They are *hidden* in the ground inside my tent, with the silver underneath (Josh. 7:20-21, emphasis added).

supports Israel, we have a chance at surviving. But the moment we withdraw our support, God is no longer bound by His covenant promise.

It is a divine principle that where ethical and moral corruption exists, judgment will fall. Because our nation is riddled with ethical and moral turpitude (immoral, shameful, vile character), illustrated in the area of bloodshed alone (the abortion issue), we have polluted the land, and invite disaster (cf. Deuteronomy 35:33). God did bring disaster on those cities that placed personal pleasures above God's decrees. Examples like Sodom and Gomorrah, the Canaanite cities, Pompeii, etc. are living proof that a nation cannot flout their sin at God and expect to get away with it.

God is calling the Christians to repentance because of this great threat that looms over our nation.

The Christian Church Must Turn From Their Wicked Ways

I have attempted to demonstrate that both covenant Israel and the Christian church are being addressed in the prayer for our nation found in 2 Chronicles 7:14. With the Christian church or the people of God in mind, what does God expect us to do? He expects us to turn from what He calls "wicked ways." Thus far, I have put labels on some of the "wicked ways;" the apostasy, the tendency toward moralism, and the partaking of the "dedicated things," but this is only an outworking of the general malaise or *apathy* that has stricken the Church.

The apathetic man in the pew has sway over a great deal in the church because this attitude is extremely infectious and it can bring down the mightiest of churches. Several words are used as synonyms for apathy. They include: indifference, complacency, passiveness, listlessness, and reluctance. In short, the apathetic man would rather somebody else perform the task God is asking him to do. And to protect this mentality, he builds an arsenal of excuses. The task may be sharing his faith with his unbelieving co-workers or neighbors, or inviting family members to church to hear an evangelist, or perhaps turning from a sin that causes others to fall. All because we are indifferent toward them. God warned His people Israel about this problem:

> Moses said to the Gadites and Reubenites, Shall your countrymen go to war while you sit there? . . . Now then, listen, you wanton creature, lounging in your security and saying to yourself, "I am, and there is none besides me" . . . Woe to you who are complacent in Zion, and to you who feel secure on Mount

Samaria . . . A curse on him who is lax in doing the Lord's work! (Nu. 32:6; Isa. 47:8; Jer. 48:10).

The only way to remedy this syndrome is for the church to repent of their apathy. John MacArthur adds to this truth: "Certainly God can bless America, but the necessary prelude to national blessing is a sweeping spiritual renewal that begins with individual repentance and faith in the Lord Jesus Christ. The revival our nation needs so badly will not occur unless we as
individuals repent."[32]

Paul taught on the difference between true and false repentance in Second Corinthians where he wrote: "Godly sorrow brings repentance that leads to salvation and leaves no regret, but worldly sorrow brings death" (7:10).

It is this sin of *apathy* that must be repented of in order for God to bless us.

---

[32]This blessing/cursing relationship regarding Israel is promised in various texts, Gen. 12:1-3; 30:27; Deut. 28; Acts 3:25; Gal. 3:8). Additionally, history attests to the law of divine retribution applied to Israel's oppressors. Those enemies include Assyria, Babylon, Medo-Persia, Greek-Macedonian and Rome. The divine retribution promised to the Arab-bloc nationsThe act of repentance toward apathy must be genuine, not false. True repentance requires that the man in the pew "change his mind" toward, or "turn away" from, this sin of apathy by recognizing it for what it is, sin. Then it must be confessed before God and followed up for their part in persecuting Israel is yet future.

with action to show God he is serious about it. False repentance is to merely acknowledge it, but have no change of heart toward the sin.

Godly sorrow or true repentance was exhibited by David when confronted by Nathan the prophet after he committed adultery with Bathsheba. This repentance is pointedly demonstrated in David's confession found in Psalm 51. By contrast, we see false repentance exhibited by the Pharaoh of the Exodus where he supposedly repented after confronted by Moses where he said: "This time I have sinned, The Lord is in the right, and I and my people are in the wrong" (Exodus 9:27).

Now we know from history that Pharaoh didn't really mean it. He did not repent, but simply professed repentance for fear of greater punishment or reprisals from God. His repentance was not genuine because he went right back to his old ways as soon as the threat was removed.[33] Whereas with David, he never committed the act of adultery again. His repentance was therefore genuine.

We need to be very clear about this issue of repentance because the outlook of the church [33]John MacArthur, *Can God Bless America?* (Nashville, TN: W Publishing Group, 2002), 29.

depends on it. Judgment can be averted if the individual Christian, and the Church at large, confesses and repents of their sin of apathy. It is to this judgment in the form of the Church losing its power that Samuel Chadwick spoke:

> The Church has lost the note of authority, the secret of wisdom and the gift of power, through persistent and willful neglect of the Holy Spirit of God. Confu-

sion and impotence are inevitable when the wisdom and resources of the world are substituted for the presence and power of the Spirit of God.[34]

Chadwick's position that the church will lose its authority, wisdom, and power out of neglect of the Holy Spirit—bringing a spirit of confusion

---

[34] The act of false repentance can be demonstrated in the penal system today. A criminal who has been caught, tried, sentenced and imprisoned is not necessarily "repentant" over their crime. They many be simply sorry that they have wronged society, or sorry that they were foolish enough to be apprehended, but rarely are they "repentant" where they have come under conviction that what they did was sinful or grieved the heart of God.

upon the church— is the foreseeable outcome of apathy. We are experiencing this impotence of the Spirit in the Church today, bearing witness of the need for the Church to repent of its apathy. Once repentance occurs, God's power will once again dominate His Church. God promised this renewal of power to Israel and His Church if they repented of their apathy: "This is what the Sovereign Lord, the Holy One of Israel says: In *repentance* and rest is your salvation, in quietness and trust is your *strength*, but you would have none of it. You said, 'No, we will flee on horses . . .'" (Isaiah 30:15-16 a, emphasis added).

Wisdom dictates that the individual in Christ's church must turn away from their apathy if the church purposes to testify for Jesus Christ in the perilous times ahead.

7
Only Then Will God Hear Our Prayer

Ichabod is a terrible epitaph for any nation or the church. The name *Ichabod* (Heb. "Where is the glory?") was given to the son of Phinehas by his wife when she heard that her husband was slain in the battle of Aphek, that Eli (her father-in-law) was dead, and that the Ark of the Covenant had been captured by the Philistines (I Samuel 4:19-22). Her lament embraced the anguish that came with the news that the enemies of God's people had triumphed, dashing her hopes and bringing on despair. Israel suffered great humiliation under Philistine oppression for the next twenty years until the Ark was recovered. At the battle of Mizpah (I Samuel 7:11-12), the Lord allowed for the reversal of the defeat at Aphek, and Samuel erected a stone monument commemorating the victory and called it *Ebenezer* (Heb. "The Lord has helped us").

I believe America is at a crossroad where God is waiting to see if His Church will call upon Him and seek His face, repent, and respond to His ardent plea so that He can pronounce the name, *Ebenezer* on us. For the Church to idly stand by and ignore God's warning—waiting for the title *Ichabod* to be placed over us—would be a violation of every principle the Bible teaches, as well as a violation of the precepts set forth by our founding fathers who wrote our Constitution.

Until our nation and the Church repents, God is saying the same thing to us that He said to Israel during the period of the Judges. When they abandoned God and did evil by serving the false gods, the Baals and the Ashtoreths, the gods of Aram, the gods of Sidon, and the gods of Moab, God "sold" them into the hands of the Philistines and the Ammonites who shattered and crushed them. They were oppressed for eighteen years by these "terrorists" until they cried out to the Lord to rescue them. But God, tired of their cyclical faith, rebellion and apostasy, replied, "Go and cry out to the gods you have chosen. Let them save you when you are in trouble (Judges 10:14).

Following the horrific assault on our nation by terrorism, did our nation or the church ask, "What is God's message?" No. We want sin without guilt and punishment. Conversely, we want the pleasures of the world while at the same time calling ourselves "Christians." But God in His mercy is longsuffering, not willing that any should perish, and accordingly, extends His grace to allow a recalcitrant nation or church to change their mind and return to Him. But there is a limit to God's patience.

This was exhibited to Manasseh, king of Judah, who performed detestable acts of idolatry, human sacrifice, divination, and witchcraft. The Bible text tells us that God spoke to Manasseh (2 Chronicles 33:10), but that *he paid no attention to His warning.* Shortly afterward the Lord sent the Assyrians who took Manasseh prisoner and led him in shackles to Babylon. His regret for sin came too late. Yes, Manasseh did ultimately repent and learn his lesson, enabling God to restore him, but because of his refusal to heed the warning, affliction did come upon him. If only he had listened to God *before*, he could have avoided God's wrath.

God Answers the Prayer of the Penitent

When the penitent pray to confess their sin, be they America, the Church, or an individual head of a family, God will withdraw His sentence of judgment. Disaster will be averted, and God will bless them beyond measure.

Prior to the fall of Jerusalem in 586 B.C., Jeremiah warned the Israelites that judgment would come if they did not repent of their national and individual sins. Then, in a demonstration of His divine mercy that could be afforded them, God asked Jeremiah to visit the Potter's house to witness an example of His sovereign mercy through the potter shaping and molding the clay on the wheel. Afterward, the word of the Lord came to Jeremiah: "Like clay in the hand of the potter, so are you in my hand, O house of Israel. If at any time I announce that a nation or kingdom is to be uprooted, torn down and destroyed, and *if that nation I warned repents of its evil, then I will relent and not inflict on it the disaster I had planned*" (Jeremiah 18:6-8, emphasis added).

The language is in the form of an anthropomorphism so that man could understand the heart of God. He would answer the prayer of the penitent by calling off the judgment they deserved. In Israel's case, they would not listen to the prophet Jeremiah. Israel did not repent, and the Babylonian's invaded their land and took them captive for seventy years.

If and when America repents, we can expect that national revival will break out, and God, being true to His promises, will destroy our enemies and heal our land. Unprecedented answers to prayer can be expected (cf. Psalm 33:12), and we will be blessed with protection and prosperity.

8
National and Individual Forgiveness of Sins

Any nation, church, or individual, that is under chastisement from the Lord can humble themselves and repent of their sin thereby receiving God's forgiveness before His wrath is executed. God, in His mercy, always gives man a chance to avoid punishment. He demonstrated this in His remedy for sin through the act of redemption first instituted through the Messianic promise to Adam, and ultimately all who would believe, in the Garden of Eden (cf. Genesis 3:15). Then again He demonstrated His desire to avoid the loss of life through repentance before the Flood of Noah; before bringing destruction on Sodom and Gomorrah; and before destroying the Assyrian city of Nineveh in the time of Jonah. These, among other examples, all point to the ultimate demonstration of forgiveness, Christ's death on the Cross. Christ said: ". . . the Son of Man did not come to be served, but to serve, and to *give his life as a ransom for many* . . . the Son of Man has authority on earth *to forgive sins*" (Mt. 20:28; Mk. 2:10, emphasis added).

The apostle Paul adds: "Be kind and compassionate to one another, forgiving each other, just as in Christ God forgave you" (Ephesians 4:32).

Clearly, God extends the opportunity to man to receive forgiveness and spiritual restoration from Him, rather than turn inward to their own strength during a time of correction. This message was made clear to the nation of Israel and speaks to the attitude facing America as well:

> The ox knows his master, the donkey his owner's manger, but Israel does not know, my people do not understand. Ah, sinful nation, a people loaded with guilt, a brood of evildoers ... they have forsaken the Lord; they have spurned the Holy One of Israel and turned their backs on him. Your country is desolate, your cities burned with fires; your fields are stripped by foreigners right before you ... when you spread out your hands in prayer, I will hide my eyes from you; even if you offer many prayers, I will not listen. Your hands are full of blood; wash and make yourselves clean. Take your evil deeds out of my sight! Stop doing wrong, learn to do right! If you are willing and obedient, you will eat the best from the land; but if you resist and rebel, you will be devoured by the sword (Isaiah 1:3-4, 7, 15-16, 19-20).

God, through the prophet Isaiah, warned Israel that He would continue to raise up enemies that would strip their land unless they had a change of heart toward Him and repented or stopped doing what was wrong and, in turn, did what was right. They professed to be God's people, yet as the ox knew his master, Israel continued in a path of sin, contrary to what God expected of His chosen, called out people. As I have shown, to a great degree, the American people and the Church as antitypes have turned their back on the Lord, and our hands are full of blood, resulting in us being loaded with guilt. The time has arrived for America and the Church to seek national and individual forgiveness for sin. This only comes about through the proper relationship with God. God made this very clear in our theme verse: "If my people, who are called by my name, will humble themselves and pray and seek my face and turn from their wicked ways, then will I hear from heaven and will forgive their sin and will heal their land" (2 Chronicles 7:14).

The Importance of Forgiveness

No book of religion, except the Bible, teaches that God completely forgives sin. Both Old and New Testament affirm this truth:

> I will heal their waywardness and love them freely, for my anger has turned away from them (Hosea 14:4).

And,

> For I will forgive their wickedness and will remember their sins no more (Jeremiah 31:34).

And,

> As far as the east is from the west, so far has he removed our transgressions from us (Psalm 103:12).

And,

> He forgave us all our sins (Colossians 3:13).

Dr. Ralph D. Curtin

Divine forgiveness in the Hebrew is rendered "to cover" or "take away." This divine act is accomplished when a nation or individual recognizes their sinfulness and confesses their sin before the Holy and Just God. He then grants us repentance and allows us to see for ourselves the terrible effect our sin has had on our inward relationship with Him and the outward effect on the world around us. Since all sin negatively affects both God and man, repentance and His forgiveness must have even greater positive effects. It is through the operation of the omnipresent, omniscient, and omnipotent Holy Spirit that this work is carried out.

The importance of forgiveness is seen when we see the affect it has on the sinner, be it a nation, a church or an individual. When Israel had their sins forgiven through the sacrificial system on the annual Day of Atonement, they rejoiced, despite the fact that it was only a temporary cleansing.

In the New Testament the author of Hebrews explains Christ's fulfillment of that feast day, whereby His sacrifice was permanent, doing away with the need for a sacrificial system:

> The blood of goats and bulls and the ashes of a heifer sprinkled on those who are ceremonially unclean sanctify them so that they are outwardly clean. How much more, then, will the blood of Christ, who through the eternal Spirit offered himself unblemished to God, cleansing our consciences from acts

that lead to death, so that we may serve the living God (9:13-14).

The effect forgiveness in Christ has on the sinner is multifaceted. There is the cleansing that brings great spiritual relief knowing that all is well between the sinner and God. There is the clearing of the conscience that relieves the sinner of guilt with its emotional and physical ramifications. There is the promise of reform that promotes encouragement to try harder. Then there is the peace and joy.

The peace of God that comes with forgiveness transcends all understanding (Philemon 4:7) while the joy of our forgiveness brings us renewed strength (Nehemiah 8:10). This peace comes from a personal relationship with God once we have received Christ as our Savior and Lord. Arriving at the place where we experience this peace and joy is quite unique from the Old Testament method. Whereas the Old Testament method of forgiveness required a blood sacrifice each year, the New Testament method simply requires the sinner to confess Christ and their sin in order for reconciliation with God to occur. This is amply explained by John: "If we confess our sins, he is faithful and just and will forgive us our sins and purify us from all unrighteousness" (I John 1:9).

Unlike the temporal lessening of hostility and happiness that comes from gratifying things in the physical world, this joy that comes from God's forgiveness is independent of any circumstance since it wells up from within our spirit, permeates our heart and becomes entrenched in our mind.

Dr. Ralph D. Curtin

That means no catastrophe, crisis, hardship or unpleasantness can rob us of it.

9
Our Land Will Be Healed

The time has come for the Christian and every God-fearing patriot in our nation to stand up and be counted for the belief that made America great. That belief is faith and trust in the Lord Jesus Christ, the Son of God. In order for our land to be healed, action must be taken to prevent the further erosion of that very faith that our forefathers believed would keep our nation from ruin. For us to do nothing will prove disastrous.

Edmund Burke (1729-1798), an outstanding orator and leader in Great Britain during the time of the Revolutionary War said: "All that is necessary for evil to triumph is for good men to do nothing."[35]

The Christian Believer, in good conscience, cannot sit idly by and allow our nation to be gradually overtaken by subversive liberal forces that undermine the very Constitution our nation was founded upon. Our nation is perched very precariously on the precipice that overlooks the chasm of doom and it is only by the sheer might of the Christian church that we will be spared being thrown headlong into its terrible maw by those who have no regard for eternal values.

This terrible truth has been attested to in recent history by Martin Niemoller:

---

[35] William J. Federer, *America's God and Country*. (Coppell, TX: Fame Publishing, 1994), 82.

> In Germany they came first for the Communists, and I didn't speak up because I wasn't a Communist. Then they came for the Jews, and I didn't speak up because I wasn't a Jew. Then they came for the trade unionists, and I didn't speak up because I wasn't a trade unionist. Then they came for the Catholics, and I didn't speak up because I was a Protestant. Then they came for me, and by that time no one was left to speak up.[36]

When the Christian church recognizes that *they* are responsible for the present condition of our nation, and that over the past two decades the Church has allowed liberalism and moralism to permeate our society and reach its tentacles down into the pulpit, then, and only then can we expect to see any relief from the divine rod of correction. Our nation will begin the healing process by first repenting of their tolerance toward sin then looking forward to reconciliation with God. The problem lies squarely with the people of God.

John Garfield (1831-1881), the 20th President of the United States proclaimed:

> Now more than ever before, the people are responsible for the character of their Congress. If that body be ignorant, reckless, and corrupt it is because the

people tolerate ignorance, recklessness, and corruption. If it be intelligent, brave and pure, it is because the people demand these high qualities to represent them in national legislature . . . . If the next centennial does not find us a great nation . . . it will be because those who represent the enterprise, the culture and the morality of the nation do not aid in controlling political forces.[37]

God's people should be expected to take the initiative and participate in any arena that will allow them to have an impact for Christ, be it a political, financial, ecclesiastical or academic platform. Charles Finney, the great American preacher of the nineteenth century proclaimed:

---

[36]Charles W. Colson, *Kingdoms In Conflict*, (Grand Rapids, MI: Zondervan Publishing House, 1987), 125.

[37]William J. Federer, *America's God and Country*. (Coppell, TX: Fame Publishing, 1994), 256.

> The church must take right ground in regards to politics . . . the time has come for Christians to vote for honest men, and take consistent ground in politics or the Lord will curse them . . . God cannot sustain this free and blessed country, which we love and pray for, unless the Church will take right ground. God will bless or curse this nation according to the course Christians take in politics.[38]

Although Finney's admonition was designed to encourage Christians to remain active in politics, the principle that the Church must be aggressively involved in every virtuous endeavor in the world around us is very clear. The Christian is not being faithful to God if they are simply sitting on the sidelines or in the bleachers observing the game. The Christian must agree to lift up the banner of Christ and march in the

---

[38] William J. Federer, *America's God and Country*. (Coppell, TX: Fame Publishing, 1994), 235.

protest parade to uphold God's honor or forfeit their rightful blessings that are promised to those who will. The Christian can no longer afford to respond with mere verbal dissent. If we are not taking the risk to defend our faith, then we are not being faithful. It's time for the Christian to put words into action. Then we can expect our nation to heal.

WHEN OUR NATION IS HEALED

We can expect that our nation will undergo a radical change when God performs the healing. The first stage of healing will involve the lifting of the plague of death we have been undergoing. The national affliction—the millions of deaths attributed to AIDS and abortion—will cease. In this regard, President Abraham Lincoln made a remarkable corollary in the middle of the Civil War when people went to him and asked, "Mr. Lincoln, sir, how much longer will this go on?"

And the President said, "I have no idea, but this is my fear; I fear God will permit it to continue until enough blood is shed North and South to equal all the blood shed by the slave master's lash."[39]

We can easily equate Lincoln's statement with the healing we can expect when our nation repents of the sinful causes that yield the deaths from AIDS and abortion. That cause is the deterioration of biblical principles and the outworking of that abandonment in our society.

At another time, March 30, 1863, at the historic event of President Lincoln's *Proclamation Appointing a National Fast Day* he said:

> And, insomuch as we know that, by His divine law, nations like individuals are subject to punishments and chastisement in this world, may we not justly fear that the awful calamity of

---

[39]*The Salt and Light Solution*, (Ft. Lauderdale, FL: Coral Ridge Ministries, 1999), 20.

> civil war which now desolates the land may be but a punishment inflicted upon us for our presumptuous sins to the needful end of our national reformation as a whole people?
>
> We have been the recipients of the choicest bounties of Heaven. We have been preserved these many years in peace and prosperity. We have grown in numbers, wealth and power as no other nation has ever grown.
>
> But we have forgotten God. We have forgotten the gracious Hand which preserved us in peace, and

multiplied and enriched and strengthened us; and we have vainly imagined, in the deceitfulness of our hearts, that all these blessings were produced by some superior wisdom and virtue of our own.

Intoxicated with unbroken success, we have become too self-sufficient to feel the necessity of redeeming and preserving grace, too proud to pray to the God that made us! It behooves us then to humble ourselves before the offended Power, to confess our national sins and to pray for clemency and forgiveness.[40]

It is apparent that Lincoln had a wonderful grasp of the Divine oracles that mandate the repentance and confession our nation must experience before God would heal our land.

Josiah, king of Judah during the divided kingdom, had a similar revelation. He was the son of a wicked father, Amon. But Josiah, fearing that God was about to bring a great disaster upon his nation for their abandonment of Him and their propensity toward evil, called upon Hilkiah the high priest to bring him

---

[40]William J. Federer, *America's God and Country*. (Coppell, TX: Fame Publishin,g 1994), 383-384.

the Book of the Law so he could see for himself what he needed to do in order to avert God's wrath. After he read the Scriptures, he tore his robes (a gesture of repentance), prayed, and wept before God over his nation's sins. His act of repentance brought a revival in Judah and out of that revival came a reprieve from the Lord who said, "I have heard you . . . your eyes will not see all the disaster I am going to bring on this place (II Kings 22:19-20).

This is who our God is. He is a God or mercy and compassion who will only bring judgment to a nation, church or individual as a last resort. And then only after His grace has been abused.

In addition to his strong opposition against abortion in America, President Ronald Reagan in the year 1980 made a bold statement regarding the healing of our nation. In his heart he knew that healing could only come from God, and without that healing, America would fall: "The time has come to turn to God and reassert our trust in Him for the healing of America ... our country is in need of and ready for a spiritual renewal ... If we ever forget that we are One Nation Under God, then we will be a Nation gone under."[41]

More than twenty-two years have passed since these words of admonishment were spoken, and yet America is still rushing furiously to fulfill this prophetic utterance of a national disaster. Lest we think for one moment that we can avoid a disaster though humanist or moralist means, great men of faith, as well as our nation's patriots, have said otherwise. Senator John Armstrong (1758-1843) expressed it this way:

> Nor is this spiritual and moral disease to be healed by a better education, a few external, transient thoughts. It requires the hand of the great Physician, the Lord Jesus Christ, by His Holy Spirit, and belief of the truth renewing the

state of mind and disposition of the heart as well, thereby leading the soul from a

---

[41] William J. Federer, *America's God and Country*. (Coppell, TX: Fame Publishin,g 1994), 528-530.

sense of fear of the wrath of God, the penalty of this broken law, and helpless in itself, to flee to the merits of Jesus, that only refuge or foundation which God hath laid in His Church, and who was made sin for us (that is, a sin-offering), that all "believers be made the righteousness of God by Him."[42]

We have seen that biblical texts, along with strong statements by heroic men of faith that have served our country well, provide many infallible proofs that our nation must undergo a spiritual healing in order for God to Bless America.

THE OUTWORKING OF THE HEALING

I have compiled a partial list of the healing that Americans can expect when we return to God:

---

[42] William J. Federer, *America's God and Country*. (Coppell, TX: Fame Publishin,g 1994), 29.

- When you and your children return to the Lord your God and obey him with all your heart and with all your soul according to everything I command you today, then the Lord your God will restore your fortunes and have compassion on you . . . . He will make you more prosperous and numerous than your fathers. The Lord your God will put all these curses on your enemies who hate and persecute you. Then the Lord your God will make you most prosperous in all the work of your hands and in the fruit of your womb, the young of your livestock and the crops of your land (Deut. 30:2-3, 5, 7, 9).

- The Lord your God will set you high above all the nations on earth. You will be blessed in the city and blessed in the country. The fruit of your womb will be blessed, and the crops of your land and the young of your livestock . . . . the Lord will grant that the enemies who rise up against you will be defeated before you.

They will come at you from one direction but flee from you in seven. The Lord will send a blessing on your barns and on everything you put your hand to. Then all the peoples of the earth will see that you are called by the name of the Lord, and they will fear you. The Lord will open the heavens, the storehouses of his bounty, to send rain on your land in season and to bless all the work of your hands. You will lend to many nations but will borrow from none. . . . you will always be at the top, never at the bottom (Deut. 28:1, 3-4, 7-8,10, 12-13).

- The Lord will keep you free from every disease. He will not inflict on you the horrible diseases you knew in Egypt, but he will inflict them on all who hate you (Deuteronomy 7:15).

Put into modern terms, we can expect God's healing to manifest itself in the following areas:

- We can expect that a cure for AIDS and other pandemic diseases that have plagued our nation will emerge.
- We can expect fewer conception and pregnancy problems. Fewer birth defects and related sexual dysfunctional conditions.
- Our nation's troubled youth will be blessed. Teen suicides and school-related tragedies will cease.

- Terrorist states will have the fear of the God of Israel placed in them. They would no sooner rise up against America than the Canaanite would come against the Israelite. We will be free from terrorist threats. Our military will have clear and decisive victories in short order.
- Crime rates will drop dramatically.
- We will no longer be a debtor nation.
- We will no longer be plagued with bizarre weather conditions (vast woodlands consumed by wildfires, earthquakes, etc.).
- God will bless our food supplies, eliminating any threat of famine. Meat recalls will stop. No one will go hungry.
- America will no longer be considered a nation filled with indulgences. The quest for hedonism and materialism will no longer dominate the American mind.
- Our domestic manufactured products (automobiles, camera equipment, etc.) will no longer be subordinate to foreign imports.
- The huge financial fortunes

that have been lost in corporate failures that have impacted on both the large and small investor will be restored.

- America will experience national, corporate, and individual prosperity.

America will never be considered a great nation because of its advances in science, technology, warfare, or business enterprise. America will not be considered a great nation because of its vast wealth of natural resources or intellectual minds. America's greatness can only be attributed to its adherence to the basic principles ordained by God in His sacred Word. Basic principles found in the Bible guided the thinking of America's patriarchs as they wrote the documents that our government with all its statutes and regulations is based upon.

The application of these basic principles can be seen in the following excerpt from George Washington's Inaugural Address to Both Houses of Congress in 1789, and his Farewell Speech of 1796:

We ought to be no less persuaded that the propitious smiles of Heaven can never be expected on a nation that disregards the eternal rules of order and right which Heaven itself has ordained. Of all the dispositions and habits which lead to political prosperity, Religion and morality are indispensable supports. In vain would that man claim the tribute of Patriotism, who should labor to subvert these great Pillars.[43]

THE SEVEN PRINCIPLES THAT MADE AMERICA GREAT[44]

Our nation cannot expect to be healed unless we revert back to the seven principles that made America great. These principles are from both Old and New Testament texts:

- The principle of the dignity of human life (Ex. 20:13; Mt. 5:21, 22). The Commandment that says, "Thou shalt not kill," is being blatantly violated in our land today. In a land that has led the world in its position regarding the dignity and value of human life, we are today allowing the murder of millions of innocent babies. We are violating a moral principle upon which this nation was built, and we are suffering the consequences of this violation.
- The principle of the tradi-

---

[43] William J. Federer, *America's God and Country*. (Coppell, TX: Fame Publishin,g 1994), 652, 661.

[44] Adapted from an extract from a publication by Jerry Falwell, *Seven Principles That Made America Great*.

tional monogamous family (Gen. 2:21-24; Eph. 5:22-33). A biblical family begins when a man legally marries a woman. Aberrant relationships such as common law or homosexual marriages are a direct violation of this principle.

- The principle of common decency (Gen. 3:7, 21; Mt. 5:27-28; Eph. 5:3-5). Common decency in a race that is fallen because of sin begins with the covering of the human body. Today pornography is a billion-dollar business in our country, being "protected" under the First Amendment. Internet, CD-ROMs, videos, and magazines portraying nudity and sexual acts have permeated our society, doing irreparable damage to the spiritual, moral, and emotional welfare of both family and individual.

- The principle of the work ethic (Gen. 3:19; Ex. 20:9-10; II Thess. 3:10). The Bible makes it clear that a man is to live by working with his hands. The result of the curse of sin upon man was that by the sweat of his brow he would earn his bread. There is a dignity in hard work, a dignity the welfare system has stripped from millions of Americans. The free enterprise system is certainly the best economic system human minds have conceived. It encourages ambition, incentive, competition, and hard work.

- The principle of the Abrahamic Covenant (Gen. 12:1-3; Rom. 11:1-2). God promised Abraham that through his seed all the families of the earth would be blessed. This is the Messianic Promise. Jesus Christ provided the fulfillment for that blessing. The Jewish people are God's chosen, with Palestine belonging to Israel. God deals with the Gentile nations in direct proportion to how they deal with Israel.

- The principle of the God-centered education (Deut. 6:4-9; Eph. 6:4). Tragedies in our nation's schools over the past three years are strong evidence of a great void in the system. It appears that since prayer and creationism have been banned, being replaced with rock idols as models and evolutionary teachings, that students have lost their sense of conscience. Moral permissiveness, drug abuses, existentialism, and academic deterioration have rushed in to fill the vacuum.

- The principle of divinely ordained establishments. (1) The home (Gen. 2:21-24; Eph. 5:22-33). (2) State or civil government (Gen. 10:32; Rom. 13:1-7). (3) Religious institution (Ex. 25:8-9, the tabernacle/temple; Mt. 16:17-19). God divinely established the institutions of the home, the state (civil government), and the church.
- The basic unit of a civilized society, the family, has come under heavy attack in the past two decades. The biblical standard of the heterogeneous marriage is no longer the traditional norm. Society is only as strong as the families within that society.
- Since God established human, civil government, to rebel against government, except when government rebels against God, is to rebel against God Himself. We are to respect authority and pray for our leaders.
- God established the church, and though it has always been under

attack by Satan, it will always remain strong and triumphant. It must always send forth the clear Gospel message: Jesus Christ was crucified, He was buried, He rose from the dead three days later, triumphant over death, hell and the grave. He is presently seated at the right hand of God and will redeem all who come to Him in faith (cf. I Cor. 15:1-6; Ps. 110:1; Heb. 1:13).

History has attested to the truth that our great American heroes were not known for their acceptance of religious beliefs that advocate terrorism or violence toward innocent civilians. They were not known for their sexual tolerance that violated biblical tenets or for "freedoms" that accepted the murdering of the innocent unborn child. They were known, however, for their bold stand against societal issues that compromised God's sacred honor and our national integrity.

Americans need role models to pattern their lives after. Like the great biblical warrior and patriarch, Joshua, America must affirm and declare before both God and man, "But as for me and my house, we will serve the Lord" (Joshua 24:15). Now is the time for the Church to be about our Father's business. We need to grow up, get up, and stand up, for Jehovah-*tsidkenu*, Jehovah our righteousness.

Then God will heal our land.

NOTES
Chapter One: Awakened America

1. Los Angeles, CA (AP) -The nation's largest Roman Catholic archdiocese could sign a $60 million settlement with dozens of alleged victims of clergy abuse within days, several attorneys told The Associated Press, AP NewsBreak; BellSOUTH editorial, 9/29/2006. Delray Beach, FL (AP)–Two Roman Catholic priests stole millions in offerings and gifts made to their parish as far back as 40 years ago, prosecutors said Thursday. Monsignor John Skehan, who was pastor at St. Vincent Ferrer Catholic Church for four decades, was arrested Wednesday night on charges that he stole $8.6 million from the church, using the money to buy property and other assets, investigators said. BellSOUTH editorial off AP, 9/28/2006.
Disregarding church law, a clergy jury in the UMC's Pacific Northwest regional unit voted to retain the ministerial credentials of Karen Dammann, a self-avowed lesbian who recently "married" her partner ("Northwest Ordinance," April 3. *Sun Sentinel*, 3/21/2004).
2. Lee Penn, *From Liberty to Leviathan, the War on Freedom,* vol. 30:2-30:3 (Berkeley, CA: Spiritual Counterfeits Project, 2006).
3. Sam Harris, *Letter to a Christian Nation* (New York,

Alfred A. Knoph, 2006).
4. Montgomery, AL. (8/27/2003, AOL) The Reverend Barry Lynn, executive director of Americans United for Separation of Church and State, added before the monument was rolled out of the rotunda [of the courtroom], "Perhaps Roy Moore will soon leave the bench and move into the pulpit, which he seems better suited for." Lynne's organization was among groups suing to remove Moore's monument.
5. America's God and Country, Encyclopedia of Quotations, Fame Publishing, Inc. Coppell TX, 226.
6. This suit was brought to the 9th Circuit Court of Appeals by atheist Michael Newdow.
7. Contrast Oregon and Washington school officials who arranged for thousands of public school students to hear a speech by Dalai Lama, a revered Buddhist religious figure (*Agape Press*, 5/9/2001).
8. Gary Bergel, quoting in part from David Barton, *America: To Pray or Not to Pray*, (Aldeo, TX: Specialty Research Associates), quoted in *America, Return to God!* (Sunnyvale, CA: Great Commission Center International), 5/ 2006.
9. "Mind Pollution," Robert W. Lee, *The New American*, 1994, 46
10. Robert W. Lee, "Mind Pollution," *The New American*, 1994.
11. Articles. news.aol.com: "Judge Bars Intelligent Design From Classrooms." 12/20/2005.

12. College Entrance Exam Board, New York. Center of Disease Control and Dept. of Health and Human Resources.
13. Data from Statistical Abstract of the United States and the Dept. of Commerce, Census Bureau.
14. Lawrence J. and Brian F. McNamee, M.D. *AIDS: The Nation's First Politically Protected Disease* (La Habra, CA: National Medical Legal Publishing House, 1988), 97.
15. Jim Nelson Black, *Loss of Faith in America*, quoted in *America, Return to God!* (Sunnyvale, CA: Great Commission Center International, 5/2006), 31.
16. Ventura CA (October 31, 2006)-Barna Update. www.barna.org.
17. Gene Edward Veith, "Gods and Country," *World Magazine*, (2003,12).
18. Lee Penn, *From Liberty to Leviathan, the War on Freedom,* vol. 30:2-30:3 (Berkeley, CA: Spiritual Counterfeits Project, 2006).
19. Articles: Bellsouth.net: "Germany Ponders Pastor's Grisly Suicide," 11/12/2006 [home.bellsouth.net/s/editorial.dll?eeid=5074495&eetype=Article].
20. Jim Nelson Black, *Loss of Faith in America,* quoted in *America, Return to God!* (Sunnyvale, CA: Great Commission Center International, 5/2006), 33.
21. David Kupelian, "The Madness of the Animal-Rights Movement," WorldNetDaily.com, 1/4/2005.
22. John MacArthur, *Can God Bless America? (*Nashville, TN, W Publishing Group, 2002), 60.

Chapter Two: Sleepwalking America

23. Barna Update: "Five Years Later: 9/11 Attacks Show No Lasting Influence on Americans' Faith." www.barna.org (9/22/2006).
24. Ibid.
25. Benjamin Netanyahu, *Fighting Terrorism*, (New York: Farrar, Straus and Giroux, 2001), 44-46.
26. Terry Eastland, *In Defense of Religious America*, Commentary (6/1981), 39 [www.commentarymagazine.com].
27. Alan Sears and Craig Osten, *The ACLU Vs. America*, (Nashville, TN: Broadman & Holman Publishers, 2005), 7, 17. Baldwin, along with the other ACLU founders, was a committed pacifist and conscientious objector to World War I. William Donohue's research disclosed that the ACLU loaned money and provided bail for many Communist Party members and Communist front organizations.
28. Ibid.
29. Ibid., 13, 9. Note: Baldwin's ally (Margaret Sanger) was a promoter of Nazi mindset.
30. Ibid., 16.
31. Ibid., 2, 5.
32. Ibid., 15.
33. The First Amendment: "Congress shall make no law respecting an establishment of religion, or prohibiting the free exercise thereof; or abridging the freedom of speech, or of the press; or the right of the people to peaceably assemble, and to petition

the Government for the redress of grievances."
34. Ibid., 28, 29.
35. Ibid., 9.
36. "Sentence Reversed Over Bible Verse,"*Cincinnati Sun-Sentinel,* 2/7/1999, 4.
37. Richmond, Virginia (November 14, 2003) AOL News, "Pagan Wins Prayer Lawsuit, Wiccan OK'ed to Open Government Meetings."
38. Dore Gold. *Hatred's Kingdom,* (Washington, D. C.: Regnery Publishing, Inc., 2003), 149.
39. Thomas Wang, *Must History Repeat Itself?* quoted in *America, Return to God!* (Sunnyvale, CA: Great Commission Center International, 5/2006), 126.
40. Barna Update: *Notional Christians.* www.barna.org (11/12/2006).

Chapter Three: The Sleeping Church

41. George Mueller, Circa 1829.
42. *Streams in the Desert* (Grand Rapids, MI: Zondervan Publishing, 1996), 354–355.
43. George Barna, *The Frog In The Kettle* (Ventura, CA: Regal Books, 1990), 158.
44. Gene Edward Veith, "Packed, But Still Empty," *World Magazine,* 8/20/2005, 24.
45. Ibid.
46. Gene Edward Veith, "Stray Pastors," *World Magazine,* 2/7/2004, 25.
47. Francis A. Schaeffer, *A Christian Manifesto*

(Wheaton, IL: Crossway Books, 1993), 19.
48. Tal Brooke, "An Update on the Emerging Church," *Spiritual Counterfeits Journal*, 30:2-30:3 (2006): 56.
49. Samuel Chadwick, *The Way To Pentecost* (Berne, IN: Light and Hope Publications, 1937), 8.
50. *Evangelical Dictionary of Biblical Theology*, (Grand Rapids, MI: Baker Books, 1996).
51. Joe Murray, "The Three R's of ABC: Rosie, Radical & Rantings." www.headlines.agapepress.org, 9/20/2006.
52. "Very PC," *World Magazine*, 6/18/2005, 35.
53. *AFA Journal*, (March 1999): 10.
54. Francis A. Schaeffer, *A Christian Manifesto* (Wheaton, IL: Crossway Books, 1993), 49
55. Francis A. Schaeffer, *Whatever Happened To The Human Race?* (Wheaton, IL: Crossway Books, 1983), 77.
56. Ibid., 65.
57. Janet L. Folger, *The Criminalization of Christianity* (Sisters, OR: Multnomah Publishers, 2005), 17.
58. Ibid., 18.
59. Ibid., 142.
60. Charles (Chuck) Colson, *Kingdoms in Conflict* (Grand Rapids, MI: Zondervan Publishing House, 1987), 125.
61. Erwin W. Lutzer, *We Must Seek God*, quoted in *America, Return to God!* (Sunnyvale, CA: Great Commission Center International, May 2006),

106.

Chapter Four: Sleeping Together

62. *New Unger's Bible Dictionary.* (Chicago, IL: Moody Press, 1988).
63. Ray C. Stedman. *Waiting For The Second Coming* (Grand Rapids, MI: Discovery House Publications, 1990), 16.
64. *New Unger's Bible Dictionary.* (Chicago, IL: Moody Press, 1988).
65. Ibid.
66. With Democrats in control of Congress, what are the prospects for the United States' pro-life aid policies in the world? Grim, said the Population research Institute's Steve Mosher. The "Mexico City Policy" first instituted by Ronald Reagan prevents U.S. aid money abroad from going to organizations that promote or perform abortions. In the 1990s Bill Clinton rescinded it, only to have Republican controlled Congress write it into law. Now Mosher expects Democrats to change the law to favor family-planning groups that have long gone without federal funding. *World Magazine*, 1/20/2007, 30.
67. *New Unger's Bible Dictionary.* (Chicago, IL: Moody Press, 1988).
68. Jim Cymbala, *Fresh Faith* (Grand Rapids, MI: Zondervan Publishing House, 1999), 93.
69. Edward Gibbon, *The Decline & Fall of the Roman Empire* (New York: Alfred A. Knoph Publishers).

70. Henry M. Morris, *The Genesis Record* (Grand Rapids, MI: Baker Books, 1976), 174.

Chapter Five: Sleeping Pills

71. Baruch Spinoza (Dutch Rationalist Philosopher, 1632-1677), quoted by Charles Colson in *Kingdoms in Conflict* (Grand Rapids, MI: Zondervan Publishing House, 1987), 75.
72. Francis A. Schaeffer, *A Christian Manifesto* (Wheaton, IL: Crossway Books, 1993), 54.
73. Humanist Manifesto I, adapted from the Humanist Manifesto as found in Vol. 6, No. 3 of *The New Humanist*, 1933.
74. Francis A. Schaeffer, *A Christian Manifesto* (Wheaton, IL: Crossway Books, 1993), 24, 26.
75. Ibid., 58.
76. Tim Lahaye, *The Battle for the Mind* (Old Tappan, NJ: Fleming Revell Company, 1980), 78.
77. Etienne Borne quote: http://en.wikipedia.org/wiki/Atheism.
78. Will and Ariel Durant, *The Lessons of History*, quoted by Charles (Chuck) Colson, *Kingdoms in Conflict* (Grand Rapids, MI: Zondervan Publishing House, 1987), 229.
79. Massimo Pigliucci, "Personal Gods, Deism, & the Limits of Skepticism," (http://psy.ucsd.edu/~ eebbesen/Psych110/SciRelig.htm) (2007).
80. Cudworth 1678.

81. Lowder 1997.
82. Pascal, Blaise, *Pensees* (1670).
83. Francis A. Schaeffer, *Whatever Happened To The Human Race?* (Wheaton, IL: Crossway Books, 1983), 95-96.
84. Pluralism: http://en.wikipedia.org/wiki/Pluralism.
85. Ibid.
86. Ibid.
87. Tal Brooke, "An Update on the Emerging Church," *Spiritual Counterfeits Journal* 30:2-30:3 (2006): 55.

Chapter Six: Sleeping Sickness

88. Alan Sears and Craig Osten. *The ACLU Vs. America* (Nashville, TN: Broadman & Holman Publishers, 2005), 143, 191.
89. Charles (Chuck) Colson, *Kingdoms in Conflict* (Grand Rapids, MI: Zondervan Publishing House, 1987), 181.
90. Ibid, 214.
91. Jim Cymbala, *Fresh Faith* (Grand Rapids, MI: Zondervan Publishing House, 1999), 181.
92. Hannah Elliott, *Accurate Definition of Evangelical" Up For DebateIn Theology, Politics*, www.goodnewsfl.org (3/2007).
93. Ray C. Stedman. *Waiting For The Second Coming* (Grand Rapids, MI: Discovery House Publications, 1990), 7, 94.
94. Lynn Vincent, "Breaking Faith," *World*

Magazine, 3/30/2002, 18.
95. Ibid.
96. Mark Bergin, "Out of the Dark," *World Magazine*, 11/18/2006, 38.
97. *Furor Over Baptist's Gay-baby Article*, www.home/bellsouth.net/s/editorial 3/14/2007.
98. http://transcripts.cnn.com/TRANSCRIPTS/0506/20/lkl.01.html (2/21/2007).
99. http://transcripts.cnn.com/TRANSCRIPTS/0506/20/lkl.01.html (2/21/2007).
100. Samuel Chadwick, *The Way To Pentecost* (Berne, IN: Light and Hope Publications, 1937), 94.
101. Allie Martin, Agape Press: www.GoodNewsFL.org. 11/2/2006.
102. "Christians 'Too Evangelical" for Catholic School." www.WorldNetDaily.com (1/ 2007).
103. George Barna, *The Frog In The Kettle* (Ventura, CA: Regal Books, 1990), 22.
104. Paraphrased from Samuel Chadwick, *The Way To Pentecost* (Berne, IN: Light and Hope Publications, 1937), 29-30.

Chapter Seven: The Looming Nightmare

105. Tim LaHaye, *How Can Revival Come?* Cited in *America, Return to God!* (Sunnyvale, CA: Great Commission Center International), 5/2006, 93.
106. Francis A. Schaeffer, *A Christian*

Manifesto (Wheaton, IL: Crossway Books, 1993), 65.
107. Vernon McLellan, *Christians In The Political Arena,* Cited in *America, Return to God!* (Sunnyvale, CA: Great Commission Center International), 5/2006, 14-15.
108. Janet L. Folger, *The Criminalization of Christianity* (Sisters, OR: Multnomah Publishers, 2005), 94.
109. Jerry Falwell, *John Ashcroft Was a Victim of 'Religious Profiling.' National Liberty Journal,* 3/2001, Volume 30 No. 3.
110. Gene Edward Veith, "Anti-Christian Paranoia," *World Magazine,* 12/2/2006, 15.
111. Edward E. Plowman, "Taking Stock," *World Magazine,* 11/13/2004, 33.
112. Gene Edward Veith, "Wandering Shepherds," *World Magazine,* 8/23/2003, 13.

Chapter Eight: Waking The Sleeping Church

113. John MacArthur, *The Truth War* (Nashville, TN: Thomas Nelson Publishers, 2007), xiv.
114. Bob Dylan, *Slow Train Coming,* New York: Special Rider Music, CBS, Inc., 1979.
115. John MacArthur, *The Truth War* (Nashville, TN: Thomas Nelson Publishers, 2007), 76.

116. Jim Cymbala, *Fresh Wind, Fresh Fire* (Grand Rapids, MI: Zondervan Publishing House, 1997), 149.
117. Bill Bright, *State of Churches is 'Scandal,'* Quoted in *Florida Baptist Witness*, 6/20/2002, 8.
118. Jim Cymbala, *Fresh Power* (Grand Rapids, MI: Zondervan Publishing House, 2001), 38.
119. John MacArthur, *The Truth War* (Nashville, TN: Thomas Nelson Publishers, 2007), 173.
120. John MacArthur, *The Truth War* (Nashville, TN: Thomas Nelson Publishers, 2007), 208.

Chapter Nine: Waking The Dead

121. Janet L. Folger, *The Criminalization of Christianity* (Sisters, OR: Multnomah Publishers, 2005), 79.
122. Charles (Chuck) Colson, *Kingdoms in Conflict* (Grand Rapids, MI: Zondervan Publishing House, 1987), 187.
123. John MacArthur, *The Truth War,* Nashville, TN, Thomas Nelson Publishers, 2007, 23.
124. Samuel Chadwick, *The Way To Pentecost* (Berne, IN: Light and Hope Publications, 1937).
125. Jay Rogers, *Charles G. Finney—The Link Between the First and Second Great Awakenings in America.* Cited in *America, Return to God!* (Sunnyvale, CA: Great Commission Center Inter-

national), 5/2006, 111.
126. Gerald McDermott, *What Can We Learn From The 18th Century Awakening.* Cited in *America, Return to God!* (Sunnyvale, CA: Great Commission Center International), 5/2006, 108-109.

Chapter Ten: Dreamland: Christian America

127. Tim LaHaye, *The Battle for the Mind* (Old Tappan, NJ: Fleming Revell Company, 1980), 38.
128. D. James Kennedy, *Christianizing America??* Cited in *America, Return to God!* (Sunnyvale, CA: Great Commission Center International), 5/2006, 92.
129. Ibid.
130. Richard Hogue, *Saints and Dirty Politics.* Cited in *America, Return to God!* (Sunnyvale, CA: Great Commission Center International), 5/2006, 127.
131. Richard Land, *Praying for Hearts Revived and a Culture Reclaimed.* ERLC (SBC) 901 Commerce St., Nashville, TN 37203-3696, 4-5.

www.ingramcontent.com/pod-product-compliance
Lightning Source LLC
Chambersburg PA
CBHW052013070526
44584CB00016B/1737